MALLUSK MEMORIALS

A RECORD OF MEMORIALS

IN THE ANCIENT GRAVEYARD

AT MALLUSK, NEWTOWNABBEY, COUNTY ANTRIM

BY THE BELFAST BRANCH

NORTH OF IRELAND FAMILY HISTORY SOCIETY

JULY 1997

ACKNOWLEDGEMENTS

Belfast Branch Project Team	Jeanne Jordan, Rosemary Sibbett, John and Flora Jackson, Robert McClung, William Stewart, Margaret Cartwright and Elizabeth Fleming.
Project leader	Jeanne Jordan
Editor	Rosemary Sibbett
Friends and helpers	James Jordan, Georgie Siberry, Joe Gracey and Arthur Templeton.
Computer consultant	Roy Sibbett
Artist	Caryl Sibbett - local Newtownabbey artist who kindly produced all the original artwork, cover designs and maps.
Newtownabbey Council	Paula Donaghy -for much help, co-operation and use of original maps. Denis Rainey (Parks Officer) and assistants, Archie Foster and Denis Esdale for help in lifting and reading fallen stones
Photographs	John Jackson, James Jordan, William Stewart, Rosemary Sibbett, and Georgie Siberry
Dr Eamon Pheonix	for permission to quote from a talk on Francis Joseph Bigger.

and thanks to anyone else who helped in any way with this project.

**SPECIAL THANKS TO THE FOLLOWING SPONSORS WHO
GENEROUSLY GAVE FINANCIAL SUPPORT AND HELP WITH
BOTH THE PUBLICATION AND THE LAUNCH OF THIS BOOK.**

NEWTOWNABBEY BOROUGH COUNCIL

THE PUBLICATION OF THIS BOOK HAS BEEN ASSISTED BY
THE ULSTER LOCAL HISTORY TRUST

FIRST TRUST BANK, GLENGORMLEY

NAMOSA / NAMBARRIE LTD

McDONALD'S, ABBEYCENTRE, NEWTOWNABBEY

STEWARTS SUPERMARKETS

MALLUSK MEMORIALS

CONTENTS

PHOTOGRAPHS

ILLUSTRATIONS

by Caryl Sibbett

GENERAL ILLUSTRATIONS

MALLUSK CEMETERY

LOOKING TOWARDS THE NEW SECTIONS

VIEW OF THE OLD SECTION

INTRODUCTION

In 1994, the Belfast Branch of the North of Ireland Family History Society produced its first publication "Carved in Stone", being a record of the memorials around the parish church at Carnmoney in Newtownabbey, County Antrim.   Following the success of this project, and with the encouragement of the Newtownabbey Borough Council, attention was focused on another burial ground in Newtownabbey, that of Mallusk.

Mallusk burying ground has a particular interest, not only for family historians, but also those interested in local and political history.   The 1798 Rebellion involving the United Irishmen drew many of its supporters from the Hydepark, Roughfort, Hightown, Lylehill and Mallusk areas, and some people who took a prominent part have been buried in this graveyard.   Jemmy Hope, members of his family, and the extensive Bigger/Biggar families have been buried here also, thus giving unique information relating to the United Irishmen.

Unlike Carnmoney, there are no visible remains of any church buildings at Mallusk, nor are there any church records relating specifically to this particular graveyard.   The grounds are clearly divided into two sections: the old burying plot, and a more modern section which has been properly planned and has graves laid out in a regular manner.   Maps of the burying ground were made available by Newtownabbey Council for this project, but it must be emphasised that the purpose of the exercise was to record the memorials and inscriptions in the grounds and not to verify or re-map graves or rights to bury in any particular plot.

The Belfast Branch is deeply indebted to the team of volunteers who so willingly undertook the inscribing and checking necessary for this project.   Particular thanks must be given to Rosemary Sibbett for her recording, desk-top publishing and editing the information contained in this publication, and to Jeanne Jordan for organising, contacting and generally making things happen. Without these two energetic and enthusiastic people this publication would not have been completed on time.

Robert McClung - July 1997

BURIAL GROUND AT MALLUSK

Nothing now remains at Mallusk graveyard of the original church that was once there. According to historical records, the Knights of St John were confirmed as the owners of "MANYBLOS" in 1231 and, in the "Taxation of Pope Nicholas" in 1306, the church of "Maynblossce" was exempted from paying taxes.

However, by 1622 the church was in ruins when the Protestant Bishop made his report. It is likely that the church fell into disuse sometime in the 1500's, possible following the dissolution of the monasteries in 1541 during the reign of King Henry V111.

In Lewis's Topographical Dictionary of Ireland, the Parish of Molusk, or Moblusk, was said to belong to the preceptory of the Knights Templar of the Parish of Templepatrick. Of their establishment in Mallusk, it was recorded that there was now no trace and that there had not been a church there since the Reformation. Tithes had not been collected for some time but the Dean for the area had said that it was the Established Church's intention to rebuild the church and collect tithes. It was noted that the inhabitants of the area were exclusively Presbyterian.

The Ordnance Survey Memoirs of 1838 (Co Antrim 1 Vol 2) for the Grange of Mallusk reported that the Parish was said to be part of the district inhabited by the Culdees of their persecution and expulsion from Northumberland in 664 AD due to their religious beliefs. This appeared to be borne out by the name of the adjoining area of Umgall, meaning "the land of strangers".

The Culdees were an ancient order of Christian monks who survived in Ireland and Scotland to about the 12th Century, when the Celtic Church to which they belonged was forced to conform to Roman practices. Some survived to the 14th century and, at Armagh, they endured until the dissolution of the monasteries in 1541.

In a footnote to the OS Memoirs, reference was made to land grants in the 4th year of the reign of James I as follows:-

"Sir James Hamilton did grant the Parish of Templepatrick and Myluske to Sir Arthur Chichester, Lord Deputy of Ireland, and 2 parts of the tithes and altarages of the church of the impropriate rectorage of Myluske ...... which were late the priorate or hospital of St John of Jerusalem in Ireland, for 15s annually."

In a further footnote, mention was made of a pamphlet on the Parish of Templepatrick. This was published in 1825 by Dr Stephenson of Belfast who noted that in the 14th or 15th centuries the Knights of St John were said to have erected the ancient church of Mallusk but that the foundations had long since been dug up. He also mentioned that under the graveyard there was an extensive cove (souterrain).

In 1995, the developer of an area adjacent to the graveyard discovered a stone lined cavity on the western side and reported his find to the appropriate authorities. On investigation, it was confirmed that the cavity was in fact part of the souterrain. The Archaeological Development Services performed a small scale excavation and found that the souterrain chamber ran beneath the graveyard wall and continued beneath the graves. A further small excavation found the original entrance to the souterrain. Some pottery fragments came to light and from these it was thought that the souterrain had been infilled in the early christian or medieval period.

The OS Memoirs also refer to a large undressed stone sunk about three feet below the surface of the adjacent ground near the west centre of the old graveyard.

Only a small portion of the stone was visible and in it was a smoothly cut circular hollow 12 inches in diameter and seven inches deep. It was assumed that this was once a baptismal font.

The stone can be seen today at No 38 in the Old section of the Graveyard.

However, archaelogists now say this is in fact a "bullaun" stone (or mortar) often associated with the grinding of meal.

The combination of the souterrain and the bullaun stone can be interpreted as evidence of the presence of an early Christian ecclesiastical site re-used in the medieval period.

It therefore seems certain that Mallusk was an important ritual site of considerable antiquity.

The Bullaun Stone

NAME VARIANTS

Family and local historians always need to be aware of the variations often used in the spelling of both family names and also place names. As can be seen in the above article, there were many changes to the name of Mallusk. It has been suggested that the original gaelic name was "Magh-an-bhloisce" meaning "plain of the congregation". In the 13th century, when the Knights of St John possessed the territory, it was known as "Manyblos" but by 1306 the "Taxation of Pope Nicholas" referred to it as "Maynblossce".

In the reign of James I it was variously known as "Moyvelusk", "Molusk", "Moybleske", "Moybluske", "Myluske and "Moyvliske". By 1657, the name had changed again to "Molisk" and twenty years later to "Moyliske". More recently, in the 1800's "Moblusk", "Molusk" and "Mulusk" were is use. This has now become the present day spelling of "Mallusk".

John and Flora Jackson

BIBLIOGRAPHY

There are many interesting publications which give information about this historic area.   For further details of this parish of Mallusk, the following books will be specially helpful:-

"Through the Ages to Newtownabbey"   Robert Armstrong   1996

Ordnance Survey Memoirs of Ireland   Institute of Irish Studies,   1990
Parishes of County Antrim 1 - Vol 2   Queen's University, Belfast.

Sentry Hill - Wm Fee McKinney   1985

In Remembrance - Francis Joseph Bigger   1927

The Town Book of the Corporation of Belfast   1892

Down and Connor - O'Laverty   c1880

"Antrim and Down in '98"   Dr Richard R Madden   1798-1887

Lewis Topographical Dictionary

We would also recommend the following helpful places to research about the area surrounding this cemetery and also the
families buried here:-

Linenhall Library, Donegall Square North, Belfast

Belfast Central Library, Royal Avenue, Belfast

Public Record Office of Northern Ireland, 66 Balmoral Avenue, Belfast

THE OLD RESURRECTION LAMP

A feature of the Old section of the graveyard, just to the right of the gate, is the ancient iron lamp stand. It used to be located in the centre of the graveyard and was used to illuminate the area. After an interment, an oil lamp would be lit in the lamp stand. Then, from an upper room of the house which stood at the gates, relatives of the deceased would take turns keeping watch for grave robbers. Often armed with guns, they watched for several weeks after the interment.

For many years, there had been a demand for a regular supply of corpses by the medical profession in Glasgow and Edinburgh and this led to the substantial increase in grave robbing.

Matters came to a head in the 1820's when the infamous pair Burke and Hare (both of Irish descent) even took to murder to obtain bodies.

Thankfully, the Government legalised the situation by passing the Anatomy Act of 1832 which effectively put an end to the dreadful trade of the body snatchers.

THE NEAREST CHURCHES

HYDEPARK WESLEYAN METHODIST CHURCH

Building started in 1828.

Completed and opened on 28 June 1829.

Cost unknown. Collection at opening £40 (worth approx £2000 today)

HYDEPARK PRESBYTERIAN CHURCH

Following requests from local families to set up a new congregation, the building started in 1862.

The present church cost £1140 and was opened on 7 December 1862.

JAMES HOPE (Honest Jemmy)   1764-1847
The Templepatrick Weaver

One of the most interesting stones in Mallusk is to the memory of James Hope and his family.

In order to get additional information which would be relevant to those interested in family history, I researched in the 'Memoirs of James Hope' contained in a publication "Antrim and Down in '98" by Dr Richard Robert Madden (1798-1887)

James Hope was born in the parish of Templepatrick, in County Antrim on 25 August 1764.   His father, John, was a native of the parish and one of the Covenanters.   The parish was inhabited by settlers from Scotland of which his grandfather was one.   Both his parents were buried at Mallusk.   He was baptised in Lylehill Presbyterian Church, had two brothers, and was brought up a Presbyterian under the ministry of Rev. Isaac Patten.

James Hope in his early working life was hired to local farmers in the Templepatrick parish - William Bell, John Gibson and John Ritchie.   Then for eight and a half years he served an apprenticeship as a weaver with a farmer who had a loom in his house.   As a journeyman weaver he worked for a man named Mullan, whose daughter Rose he married.   Rose's brother, Luke Mullan, was involved with the United Irishmen and is described as having "painted the flags" when the Belfast Battalion of Volunteers celebrated the taking of the Bastille.

HOPE FAMILY TREE

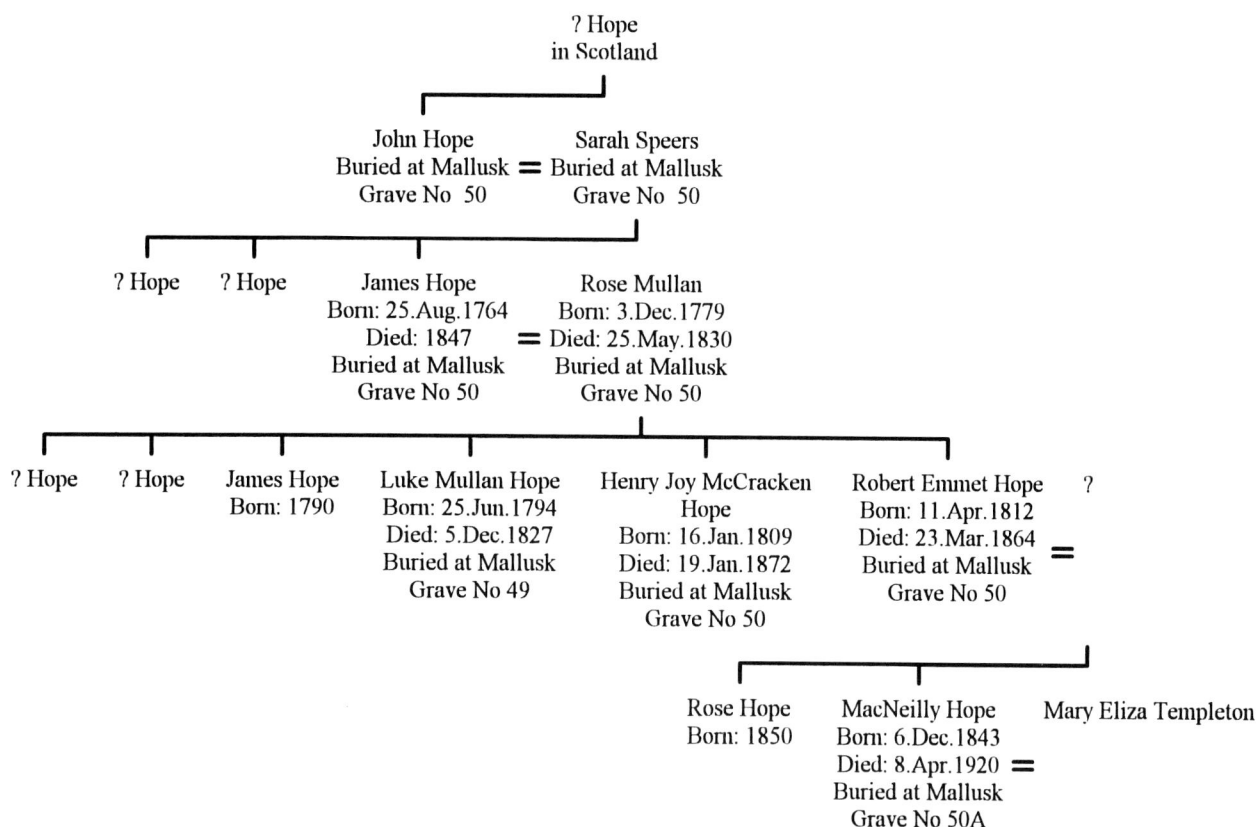

```
                                        ? Hope
                                      in Scotland
                          ┌──────────────────────┐
                      John Hope              Sarah Speers
                  Buried at Mallusk  =  Buried at Mallusk
                     Grave No 50           Grave No 50
         ┌──────────┬──────────┬──────────────────┐
      ? Hope     ? Hope    James Hope          Rose Mullan
                            Born: 25.Aug.1764   Born: 3.Dec.1779
                            Died: 1847     =    Died: 25.May.1830
                            Buried at Mallusk   Buried at Mallusk
                            Grave No 50         Grave No 50
  ┌───────┬───────┬────────────┬──────────────┬──────────────────┐
? Hope  ? Hope  James Hope  Luke Mullan Hope  Henry Joy McCracken  Robert Emmet Hope   ?
               Born: 1790  Born: 25.Jun.1794     Hope            Born: 11.Apr.1812
                           Died: 5.Dec.1827   Born: 16.Jan.1809  Died: 23.Mar.1864  =
                           Buried at Mallusk  Died: 19.Jan.1872  Buried at Mallusk
                           Grave No 49        Buried at Mallusk  Grave No 50
                                              Grave No 50
                                       ┌──────────┬──────────────────┐
                                   Rose Hope   MacNeilly Hope    Mary Eliza Templeton
                                   Born: 1850  Born: 6.Dec.1843
                                               Died: 8.Apr.1920  =
                                               Buried at Mallusk
                                               Grave No 50A
```

Hope's connection with politics began in the Roughfort Corps of Volunteers, and in June 1795 he was initiated into the Hightown Society of United Irishmen. When a deputation from Belfast formed the Mallusk Society, he became a member and was the delegate for Belfast. He was employed in 1796, 1797 and the spring of 1798 and again in 1803 as an emissary, going from place to place throughout the country, organising the people.

During the 1798 rebellions, James Hope played a prominent part in the battles which were fought in Antrim and Ballymena. In his memoirs, Hope recounts that he had refused to accept command but he was in the front rank of eighteen men. The Roughfort Volunteers led the column to Antrim followed by those from Templepatrick and Carnmoney and some from Killead. He was closely connected with the most famous leaders of the United Irishmen namely Henry Joy McCracken, Rev Steele Dickson, Robert Emmet and Thomas Russell.

In his memoirs, he stated that in 1803 "I quitted Dublin and settled down to work in Westmeath. We had then four children - three in Dublin and one in the North - my wife was ill having attended our youngest child who was ill of the small pox." In 1845, Hope wrote that he had four children "who grew up, two of whom are now living".

James Hope died in 1847 and was buried in Mallusk graveyard. Remarkably today, three memorial stones to this interesting family can still be seen at Numbers 49, 50 and 50A in the Old part of the graveyard. No 49 contains the remains of his son Luke M Hope and No 50A the remains of his grandson MacNeilly Hope - described as "the last of his stock".

Robert McClung

**THE BADGE
OF THE
SOCIETY OF
UNITED IRISHMEN
OF BELFAST**

GRAVE NO 50 AND GRAVE NO 49

FRANCIS JOSEPH BIGGER 1863 - 1926

Francis Joseph Bigger was the seventh son of a seventh son.   He was a lawyer, historian, archaeologist, ecumenist, a man of letters, and an Irish language enthusiast.   He supported home industries and also set up an Irish College on Rathlin Island.

The family came from Scotland in the 1650's and settled near Mallusk.   There is a townland called Biggerstown.   His mother was Mary Jane Ardery from Banbridge.   His house "Ardrigh" which may have been named after her, was beside the Shaftesbury Inn on the Antrim Road, Belfast.   He was influenced by his paternal grandfather David who supported the United Irishmen, and he was also influenced by his cousin Joseph Biggar, an MP for Cavan, who had businesses in Belfast The latter was responsible for the use of the Parliamentary device called a filibuster.

Francis Joseph was educated at Royal Belfast Academical Institution (his grandfather was a founder) and at Queens College (now University) where he studied law. As a young lawyer, he visited Dublin and developed an interest in archaeology and history. By 1887, he was working in a firm in Donegall Street but gradually became more involved in the Belfast Naturalist's Field Club of which he was secretary and then chairman until 1903.   He travelled extensively throughout the country and knew something about every parish in Ireland. He edited The Ulster Journal of Archaeology which published his work.

He had a great love of Irish customs and language. He supported the retention of Irish place names. He often visited Waterfoot, Co Antrim to meet Irish speakers. He helped found the Glens Feis. In 1904, he founded the G.A.A. in Antrim and presented a shield for hurling. He was a prominent member of the Gaelic League founded by Douglas Hyde, a fellow Protestant. Around 1904, he met Roger Casement who often stayed in his house recovering from bouts of malaria. Casement left his papers to Bigger but when Bigger and friends opened the papers after Casement's death, they decided to burn them.

Bigger restored Jordan's Castle in Ardglass which like his Belfast home became a centre for poets, musicians and writers including Francis McPeake, the piper from Donegal. During his life he acquired an extensive library which is now in Belfast's Central Library.

When Henry Joy McCracken's remains were exhumed from St George's church, they were kept in Bigger's home until he re-interred them in Clifton Street graveyard where McCracken's sister Mary Anne was buried. Bigger had a large Mourne granite slab placed on St Patrick's grave in Downpatrick. He often used his own money to restore crosses and graves. F. J. Bigger did not forget the poor. He left money in his will for the needy. He built labourers' cottages some of which are in Sally Gardens, Glengormley. He acquired a local inn, the Crown and Shamrock, to make it a temperance house. He enjoyed pomp and ceremony and was an active Freemason.

Although interested in Irish affairs, he distanced himself from any hint of violence and after 1921, he wrote less on politics and retained a hope for re-unification. In 1970 a bomb destroyed the cross on his grave. J. Campbell , a friend and poet wrote of him:

"I think I see him now, as in his prime, ... ".
"A brown faced, quiet mannered, human man,
Whose noble mind was mirrored in his eye:
Who loved his people and the land that bore him".

Margaret Cartwright

(from a talk given by
Dr Eamon Pheonix)

"Ardrigh" the home of
Francis Joseph Bigger

The broken granite celtic memorial to the memory of Francis Joseph Bigger at Grave No 15E Old Section

During the recent troubles an explosion rocked this grave and destroyed the celtic cross just leaving the base as shown above. The wording on the stone is:-

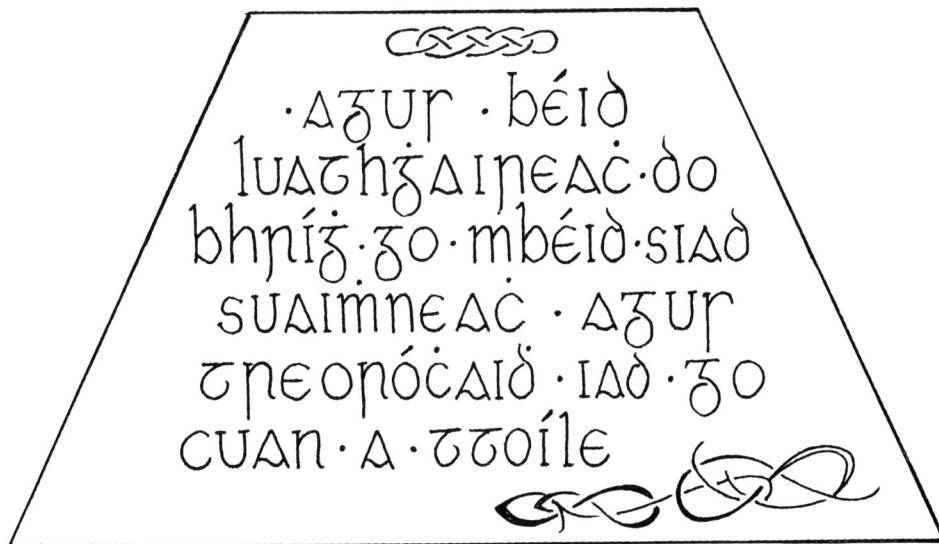

·aʒuſ · béið
luaⱦ͡ʒaiɲeaċ·ðo
bhɲíʒ·ʒo·mbéið·siað
suaimɲeaċ · aʒuſ
ⱦɲeoɲóċaið·iað·ʒo
cuan·a·ⱦⱦoíle

Francis Joseph Bigger

The Gaelic inscription given here on the remains of the stone is the 30th verse of Psalm 107:-

"Then they are glad, because they are at rest;
and so He bringeth them into the haven where they would be."

19

THE SECRET STONE
(see stone 5E old section).

Written and researched by William Stewart

Whilst recording the monumental inscriptions at Mallusk cemetery, I noticed a rough portion of stone partly hidden behind a headstone.

Upon investigation, it proved to be a complete headstone with a shaped top, hidden by undergrowth, lying sideways between the first stone and a large tree.

I called Mr Bob McClung, another member of our team, and together we worked to clear the briars, and dig out stony debris from a very narrow space, in which we could feel some lettering on the stone. Encouraged by this, we laboured on but could not free the stone as it was stuck fast.

We did, however, at last make out some of the wording

"James Bigger who departed this life 11th .... 1838 aged 87 years .... Volunteer .... Antrim on 7th June 1798"

What a find! This was someone who took part in the Battle of Antrim during the 1798 Rebellion!

We already knew that other United Irishmen were buried in Mallusk, but here was further information which had long been forgotten, by accident or design. So who was this man and would it be possible to learn more about him?

I decided to investigate and found my first clue in "The Town Book of the Corporation of Belfast" where we read on page 323, **"James Bigger was one of the earliest volunteers and a delegate at Dungannon in 1782".**

Then the book mentions a William Bigger, whose son Matthew was a Colonel on the Irish side at the Battle of Antrim. Also David Bigger, who started the Carnmoney Cotton Printing Mill, was a founder of the Linenhall Library and was a "United Irishman".

All the relationships were not shown, so I turned to church records: - namely those of Carnmoney Presbyterian Church. As our **James died in 1838 aged 87 years, he should have been born about 1751** and sure enough under baptisms was recorded:-

28 July 1751	**James, son of William Bigger**	also
13 January 1754	Joseph, son of William Bigger	

The list of baptisms was not complete due to a gap of 8 years. The old session books were in poor condition but very fortunately, that tireless worker and historian, Mr William Fee McKinney, had deciphered and copied them, also building up scores of family trees of Carnmoney people. From these and other sources, we learn the following facts:-

Mr William Bigger of Biggerstown, baptised 30 October 1718, died 1788,
married Mary Finlay 29 July 1746, she was born 1724 and died 1808.

They had nine children as shown below

1	John	Bigger	born	1747		died 1796
2	Samuel	Bigger	born	1749	married Isabella Fulton	died 1838
3	**James**	**Bigger**	**born**	**1751**	**unmarried**	**died 1838**
4	Joseph	Bigger	born	1754	unmarried	died 1792
5	Alexander	Bigger	born	1756	unmarried	died 1821
6	William	Bigger	born	1758	married Sarah Stormont	
7	David	Bigger	born	1760	married Margaret McNeilly	died 1818
8	Janet	Bigger	born	1764	married Hugh Giffen	died 1853
9	Matthew	Bigger	born	1771	married Letitia Bigger	died 1848

According to various reports, the Bigger families are descended from three brothers from Nithsdale, north of Dumfries in Scotland who settled in Belfast approximately 1640 - 1650 and also at Biggerstown, now Hightown, in the parish of Carnmoney.   This is confirmed by wording on a headstone in Carnmoney parish church graveyard - see "Carved in Stone" the first publication of The North of Ireland Family History Society which gives a record of the inscriptions at Carnmoney.

They were successful in various businesses and issued the following trade tokens.

BIGGER TRADE TOKENS 1657 - 1667

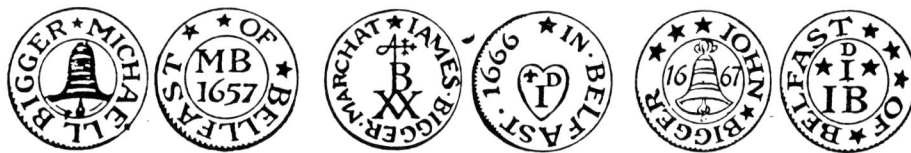

MICHAEL   JAMES   JOHN

Details of the latter years of our James Bigger remain sparse except to say that he was unmarried and died in 1838 but it is satisfying to find out exactly who he was and to preserve the details which we were able to discover in our research.

(see our brief Bigger family tree overleaf which shows how "our secret stone" fits into the picture)

MAIN INSCRIPTION LIST

ALL INSCRIPTIONS ARE INDEXED BY SURNAME
AND ALL SURNAMES MENTIONED ON STONES ARE INCLUDED

THE SOCIETY HAS TRANSCRIBED AND THEN CHECKED ALL THE INFORMATION
AS CAREFULLY AS POSSIBLE AND THEREFORE, WE SINCERELY HOPE
THAT ANY ERRORS ARE MINIMAL.

EXAMPLES

ORDINARY INSCRIPTION

SURNAME	DESCRIPTION OF STONE WHERE APPROPRIATE	GRAVE NUMBER
	INSCRIPTION	

ADDITIONAL SURNAMES

SURNAME	SEE MAIN SURNAME	GRAVE NUMBER

NO STONE BUT NAME ON MAP

SURNAME	NO STONE - ONLY NAME ON MAP	GRAVE NUMBER

THE MAP REFERRED TO IN THE ABOVE TYPE OF RECORD IS THE ORIGINAL
NEWTOWNABBEY COUNCIL MAP KINDLY LOANED TO US.   THE GRAVES IN THE
NEW SECTIONS HAVE PROPER NUMBERS GIVEN BY NEWTOWNABBEY COUNCIL
BUT IT PROVED TOO DIFFICULT TO DETERMINE WHICH NUMBER REFERRED TO
WHICH HEADSTONE SO IT WAS NECESSARY FOR THIS PROJECT FOR THE SOCIETY
TO NUMBER THE NEW SECTIONS AS   A-1   TO   A-14.

| ADAIR | white marble stone | A-14 Section |

ADAIR
in loving memory of a dear wife and mother
Annie died 23 November 1982 also her devoted husband
Samuel died 4 February 1992

| ALEXANDER | grey granite stone and surround | A-11 Section |

ALEXANDER
erected by Elizabeth Alexander in loving memory of her husband
William John who departed this life 15 March 1901 also the above
Elizabeth Alexander who died 2 September 1933
Till the day breaks
Left edge
also their son James Finlay died 6 January 1965
Right edge
also two children who died in infancy and were interred in Carnmoney
also their daughter Isabella who died 24 December 1949

| ALEXANDER | tall limestone | No 058 OLD Section |

erected by Agnes Alexander in memory of her beloved husband
David Alexander who died 22 June 1888 aged 51 years
also in loving memory of our dearly beloved daughter
Lily who departed this life 19 March 1906
the above named Agnes Alexander (MacAuley) died 24 October 1929
also their daughter Margaretta died 14 July 1949
Thy will be done.
on map - Agnes Alexander

| ALEXANDER | tall black obelisk | No 059 OLD Section |

erected by James Alexander, Roughfort, in loving memory of his wife
Margaret who died 29 January 1898 aged 70 years
also the above James Alexander who died 19 March 1927 aged 85 years
also his wife Agnes Sarah who died 16 October 1944 aged 77 years
also his sons Joseph Thoborn who died 4 February 1919 aged 14 1/2 years
Lower Panel
James died 3 July 1931 as a result of an accident aged 27 years
on map - James Alexander

| ALEXANDER | large granite stone in surround | No 060 OLD Section |

in loving memory of our father and mother
Robert Alexander died 23 June 1929
Mary Jane Alexander died 14 April 1952 also their daughters
Mary Jane died 22 May 1905
Janet Agnes died 21 January 1925
Elizabeth Alexander died 27 February 1961
Thomas J Alexander died 11 March 1970
William Alexander died 22 November 1970
Elizabeth Alexander died 8 January 1973
Robert J Alexander died 21 February 1973
Alexander C Alexander died 27 May 1975
on map - David Cowan Alexander

| ALLEN | see Finlay | A-4 Section |

| ANDERSON | grey marble | A-2 Section |

ANDERSON
in loving memory of my dear wife
Jane (Jean) who died 6 March 1976

| ANDERSON | see Mitchell | A-3 Section |

| ANDERSON | black marble stone and surround | A-5 Section |

ANDERSON
in loving memory of a devoted husband and father
Arthur who died 5 March 1979 also his dear wife
Mary who died 22 June 1984
Asleep in Jesus
Square black vase - Arthur

ANDERSON   angel on pillar and surround   A-5 Section

Front
in loving memory of
David Anderson who died 7 July 1947 also his mother
Margaret J Anderson who died 14 February 1952 also her daughter
Helen who died 12 March 1989
Left Side
Robert Mawhinney died 17 August 1934 and his wife
Ellen died 1 August 1940 and their daughter
Agnes died 29 June 1900

ANDERSON   black urn   A-8 Section

ANDERSON
in loving memory of John 15 December 1965

ANDERSON   black marble stone   A-13 Section

ANDERSON
in loving memory of a devoted husband and father
John died 16 June 1973 also a beloved wife and mother
Agnes (Ida) died 18 January 1995

ANDERSON   white marble stone in railings   No 011 OLD Section

in memory of Agnes dearly beloved wife of John Anderson, Doagh,
who died 6 February 1929 also their dear daughter
Elizabeth who died 25 March 1912 also the above
John Anderson J.P. who died 1 November 1962

ANDERSON   black marble stone   No 048 OLD Section

ANDERSON
in loving memory of James died 5 September 1953 also his wife
Margaret died 30 October 1991
on map - Wm Anderson

ANDERSON   white carved marble stone   No 048A OLD Section

erected by William Anderson in memory of his father
Thomas Anderson who died 4 May 1877 aged 66 years also his sister
Margaret who died 27 April 1885 aged 36 years and his mother
Isabella who died 16 November 1885 aged 75 years
on map - Wm Atwell

ARCHBOLD   black stone   A-14 Section

ARCHBOLD
in loving memory of John James (Ian)
a beloved husband and father died 2 July 1989
Peacefully sleeping

ARCHER   black marble stone and surround   A-13 Section

ARCHER
treasured memories of William (Billy)
husband of Dorothea died 23 November 1979

ARCHER   grey granite stone and surround   A-13 Section

ARCHER
in loving memory of my dear husband and our beloved father
David Archer who passed away 16 March 1972 also his dear wife
and our beloved mother Adelaide Archer who passed away 12 May 1982
At rest

ARMOUR   black marble stone   A-6 Section

ARMOUR
in loving memory of my dear husband
Jack died 1 November 1954 also his mother
Sarah died 20 April 1963 also his father
John died 21 March 1975 also
Isabella dear wife of Jack died 13 December 1988
At rest

ARMSTRONG	square black marble vase	A-2 Section

CONNIE ARMSTRONG

ARMSTRONG	marble stone and surround	A-3 Section

ARMSTRONG
in loving memory of
James died 2 April 1962 also his wife
Elizabeth died 12 March 1966

ARMSTRONG	headstone	A-13 Section

ARMSTRONG
loving memories of Robert Dubois
my dear brother died 6 July 1973
Till the day dawn

ATWELL	see Anderson	No 048A OLD Section

BAILIE	grey vase	A-11 Section

BAILIE   and McCLEAN

BAIRD	black surround	A-13 Section

BAIRD
in loving memory of George died 15 March 1972 also his dear
wife and our beloved sister Ellen died 28 September 1977
Love's last gift - remembrance

BARBOUR	square black vase	A-2 Section

BARBOUR

BARBOUR	white granite stone and surround	A-7 Section

in loving memory of our dear brother
Robert (Bob) Barbour died 17 March 1971
his sister and our darling mother
Emily McKnight died 8 September 1972
Ours to remember

BARKLEY	painted stone with emblem	No 091 OLD Section

erected in memory of William Barkley who died 31 October 1823 aged 55 yrs
his wife Margaret died 15 April 1839 aged 65 years
John Barkley died 6 November 1855 aged 53 years
his wife Jeanette died 25 January 1879 aged 74 years
on map - Wm Barkley

BARNETT	see McCrea	A-2 Section

BARRON	see Fearn	A-2 Section

BASKIN	see Finlay	A-4 Section

BATES	dual black marble stone	A-9 Section

BATES
in loving memory of
Thomas died 29 September 1918 also his sons
John died 8 March 1947
Thomas died 3 May 1948 and his daughter
Kathleen died 19 September 1956
Second stone
our devoted mother Hannah died 2 February 1992
dear wife of John

BEATTIE	grey stone and surround	A-9 Section

BEATTIE
in loving memory of a dear husband and father
Samuel died 21 March 1969

BEGGS	see Woods	A-8 Section

BELL	vase	A-3 Section

BELL

BERKLEY	see Bigger	No 015F OLD Section

BIGGAR	grey stone	No 095 OLD Section

Side 1
erected by William Biggar of Hightown in memory of his wife
Elizabeth who departed this life on 4 August 1837 aged 71 years
Side 2
here lies the body of James Boyd of Belnabernice parish of Templepatrick
who departed this life 8 February 1804 aged 59 years
also Janet Boyd his daughter who died young
Now, reader, pause attend to me and let the busy world go by
Thou hopest tomorrows sun to see, Alas last evening so did I
O fly to Jesus Christ in time. Thy case admits of no delay
Hate every Saviour piercing crime. Take up thy cross and come away
Your time is an uncertain span. Prepare to meet thy God, o man.
on map - Mrs Biggar

BIGGAR	no stone	No 111 OLD Section

on map - David Biggar

BIGGER	black marble stone and surround	A-2 Section

BIGGER
in loving memory of Edward died 2 March 1970
The Lord is my shepherd

BIGGER	see Parks	A-3 Section

BIGGER	black stone	A-3 Section

BIGGER
in loving memory of our dear parents
Robert died 15 April 1950
Mary E died 24 December 1976
The Lord is my shepherd

BIGGER	see Scott	A-6 Section

BIGGER	limestone and railings	A-6 Section

BIGGER
in loving memory of Samuel beloved husband of Jane Bigger
died 18 January 1951 also the above Jane Bigger died 13 June 1952

BIGGER	white marble and iron surround	A-6 Section

erected by Andrew J Bigger
in affectionate remembrance of his dearly loved wife
Margaret who died 1 January 1948 also the above
Andrew J Bigger who died 13 May 1956
Thy will be done

| BIGGER | black marble stone and surround | A-9 Section |

BIGGER
erected by Joanna Bigger
in loving memory of her husband Isaac who passed away 17 July 1935
also the above Joanna Bigger died 29 April 1954
Blessed are the pure in heart

| BIGGER | black marble stone | A-13 Section |

BIGGER
in loving memory of my dear husband
Isaac died 7 November 1990

| BIGGER | black marble and surround | A-13 Section |

in loving memory of my dear husband and our devoted father
Johnston who died 6 July 1978
Abide with me

| BIGGER | grey granite - double | A-13 Section |

BIGGER
in loving memory of a devoted wife and grandmother
Greta who died 30 January 1986 also her husband
William a devoted father and grandfather who died 28 November 1986
treasured parents of Beryl and Linda
Peace, perfect peace

| BIGGER | grey granite - double | A-13 Section |

erected by Wm Bigger in memory of our sister
Eileen McCleery who died 11 September 1978
also her husband Billy who died 1 December 1978
At rest

| BIGGER | black marble | A-13 Section |

BIGGER
in loving memory of our dear father
Thomas died 18 January 1972 also our dear mother
Emily died 29 February 1972
Always in our thoughts

| BIGGER | black stone and surround | A-13 Section |

BIGGER
in loving memory of a devoted husband and father and grandad
Kenneth died 2 August 1987 also dearly beloved grandson
Gary died 4 December 1989 aged 10 years
URN Ken - in loving memory of
BOOK - in loving memory of our very special son Gary Fulton
VASE - in memory of our daddy

| BIGGER | grey granite | A-14 Section |

BIGGER
erected by Edmund Bigger in loving memory of
Hazel died 24 April 1987 aged 16 years

| BIGGER | upright stone | No 005C OLD Section |

erected to the memory of Letitia Bigger wife of Matthew Bigger of Hightown
who departed this life 11 June 1843 aged 74 years also the said
Matthew Bigger who departed this life 24 May 1848 aged 78 years also
Sarah Bigger their daughter who died 7 November 1839 aged 30 years also
Samuel Bigger their son who died 3 February 1866 aged 65 years also
Margaret Ann George their grand daughter who died 22 Dec 1859 aged 11 years
James George died 28 May 1869 aged 59 years also his wife
Jeanette Bigger died 11 April 1889 aged 81 years
William Bigger died 30 December 1874 aged 77 years

BIGGER   stone fallen behind 005B   No 005E OLD Section

In memory of James Bigger
who departed this life 11th ... 1838 aged 87 years
for many years he was ....
volunteer and rendered good .... (service?)
to the cause of freedom. He ...
at Antrim on 7 June 1798 ....
all times upheld the honour ...
native land ....
Far dearer the grave or the prison
Illumed by one patriot name
Than the trophies of all who live
On liberty's ruin to fame
on map - James Bigger

BIGGER   headstone in railings   No 015A OLD Section

Erected by William F Bigger in memory of his mother
Margaret Bigger who died 11 August 1831 aged 32 years
also his sister Anne who died 4 March 1843 aged 19 years
also in memory of
Mrs Agnes Lindsay who died 31 December 1893 aged 65 years

BIGGER   fallen stone in railings   No 015B OLD Section

erected by Matthew Bigger of Mallusk in memory of his daughter
Ann who died 25 March 1826 aged 7 years also his daughter
Agnes who died 26 December 1826 aged 19 years also the above named
Matthew Bigger who died 5 April 1833 aged 63 years also his son
Andrew who died July 1838 aged 19 also his wife
Annie who died June 1859 aged 80 years
on map - Thomas & Wm J. Bigger

BIGGER   granite stone with celtic decor   No 015C OLD Section

in loving memory of Maude Coulter Warwick wife of
Sir Edward Coey Bigger, M.D. who died 5 February 1925
Edward Coey Bigger Knight. M.D. who died 1 June 1942 aged 81 years

---

BIGGER   granite stone with celtic decor   No 015D OLD Section

in memory of Frederic Charles Bigger ISO
10.2.60 - 15.6.44 and also of
Margaret McNeilly Bigger
20.6.65 - 19.3.40

BIGGER   broken granite celtic memorial   No 015E OLD Section

Agus béid
luachgaireac do
bhrig go mbéid siad
suaimneac agus
treorócaid iad go
cuan a-ttoile
Francis Joseph Bigger
During the recent Troubles an explosion rocked this grave and destroyed the
celtic cross. The Gaelic inscription - given above - on the remains of the
stone is the 30th verse of the Psalm CV11:
"Then they are glad, because they are at rest;
and so He bringeth them into the haven where they would be."

BIGGER   granite stone with celtic decor   No 015F OLD Section

in loving memory of Samuel Ferguson Bigger Lt. Colonel, I.M.S
who died 2 February 1931 also his wife
Evelyn Alice Berkley
who died 13 August 1951 aged 80 years

BIGGER   low granite stone   No 015G OLD Section

Joseph Warwick Bigger M.D.,F.R.C.P.I.
11 September 1891 - 17 August 1931

BIGGER	decorated limestone	No 135 OLD Section

erected by John J Bigger in memory of
his father Samuel Bigger died in 1850
and his brother Joseph died in 1860
and his mother Susan Bigger died in 1895
his brother Matthew died in 1896
his sister Hannah died in 1902

BIGGER	black marble stone	No 178A OLD Section

BIGGER
in memory of Samuel died 22 February 1975 beloved husband of
Ellen Jane died 21 October 1978 also their son
Trevor died 5 March 1985

BIGGER	black marble stone	No 178B OLD Section

BIGGER
in loving memory of Ernest died 18 December 1990
also black vase "Uncle Ernie"

BIGGER	small white marble stone	No 178C OLD Section

BIGGER

BIGGER	grey headstone	No 178D OLD Section

At the top of the stone is an inscribed London Scottish insignia
14425908 Private T Bigger
London Scottish
8 December 1947 aged 23 years
Carved cross
Remembered always by his wife and baby daughter
At rest

BIRKMYRE	see Rankin	A-8 Section

BIRKMYRE	flat white marble stone	No 005D OLD Section

erected by Margaret I Birkmyre in memory of her husband
Samuel Birkmyre, Craigarogan, died 12 November 1897 also the above
Margaret I Birkmyre died 21 October 1929

BLACK	see Platt	A-11 Section

BLACK	no stone	No 045 OLD Section

on map - James Black

BLACK	Small limestone	No 046A OLD Section

here lyes the body of John Black son to Joseph Black
who died the 1 day of January 1766 aged 23 years
on map - S Black

BLACK	no stone	No 047 OLD Section

on map - Mgt and Jas Black

BLAIN	double black stone and surround	A-2 Section

BLAIN
precious memories of Joseph a darling husband
and devoted father died 27 February 1992
Wishing we were together
black vase - Joey
black vase - Baby Joseph died 12 October 1952

BLAIN	grey marble stone	A-6 Section

BLAIN
cherished memories of a devoted husband and father
Thomas McNeilly died 14 September 1979 also his brother
Hamilton died 26 May 1972 also
Esther beloved wife of Thomas died 2 December 1990
Forever remembered

BLAIR	black marble vase	A-2 Section

BLAIR
Edward 16.3.80

BLAIR	see Gordon	A-11 Section

BLAIR	white marble stone	No 005A OLD Section

in loving memory of my dear wife and mother
Sarah J Blair died 18 October 1955 also her loving husband
and my dear father William John Blair died 16 August 1964
Until the day break.

BLAIR	white stone	No 064 OLD Section

erected by John Blair in memory of his grandson
Samuel Blair who died in infancy 1887 also his wife
Sarah who died 15 February 1899 aged 74 years also the above
John Blair who died 24 February 1901 aged 79 years also his son
Samuel who died 10 August 1920 aged 69 years and
Hannah wife of last named who died 3 May 1931 aged 87 years also their son
John T Blair died 1 December 1946 aged 71 years also his wife
Agnes (Cis) died 9 February 1959

BLAIR	small grey stone with RAF crest	No 065 OLD Section

Per ardua ad astra
Flight Lieutenant J C Blair
Pilot
Royal Air Force
10 March 1945 aged 31 years
Carved cross
"Till morning dawns
and shadows flee away"
on map - John Blair

BLAIR	no stone	No 078 OLD Section

on map - Kennedy Blair

BOAL	see Kerr	A-11 Section

BOSTON	white marble and iron surround	A-2 Section

in loving memory of our dear mother
Elizabeth Boston, Ballyhenry died 20 December 1935
also her daughter Isabella Wylie died 29 October 1961

BOSTON	stone and surround	A-13 Section

BOSTON
in loving memory of my dear husband and our devoted father
Thomas who departed this life 18 February 1979 aged 76 years
also his loving wife Margaret who departed this life
15 September 1991 aged 81 years

BOSTON	grey granite	A-13 Section

Wilfred Wyley Boston
1920 - 1971
also his wife Mary (Molly) Miskimmin nee Caruth
1920 - 1994

BOSTON	no stone	No 022 OLD Section

on map - John Boston

BOVILL	black marble stone and surround	A-2 Section

BOVILL
in loving memory of our dear parents
James died 3 June 1963
Esther died 7 January 1975 also our dear brother
Stuart died 14 June 1973
At rest

BOYCE	marble stone and surround	A-3 Section

BOYCE
in loving memory of my dear husband
Norman died 10 March 1974 also his wife
Margaret died 20 February 1986

BOYD	see Martin	A-2 Section

BOYD	small vase	A-2 Section

BOYD

BOYD	grey surround	A-3 Section

BOYD
in loving memory of a beloved husband and father
Samuel T Boyd who died 26 June 1962

BOYD	headstone & 2 vases in surround	A-5 Section

the family burying ground of Robert Boyd
and on vases - BOYD

BOYD	see Woods	A-8 Section

BOYD	see Biggar	No 095 OLD Section

BROLLY	grey marble stone	A-13 Section

BROLLY
treasured memories of a devoted husband and father
Sam died 2 February 1979
Memorial urn - Brolly, Sam died 2 February 1979

BROTHWELL	see Platt	A-11 Section

BROWN	headstone and surround	A-3 Section

BROWN
in loving memory of our dear parents
Margaret Jane nee Hamilton who died 2 June 1962 and
Alan Nesbitt Brown who died 2 February 1963

BROWN	granite stone and surround	A-5 Section

BROWN
in loving memory of
James beloved husband of Mary Brown, Hydepark
who died 23 March 1943 also the above
Mary who died 13 October 1966

CARSON   granite stone   A-8 Section

CARSON
Emily McBirney beloved wife of Fred Carson and mother of Sean
died 14 May 1921 aged 35 years

CARSON   headstone and black urn   A-13 Section

in loving memory of a dear husband and father
John who died 25 October 1930 also his dear daughter
Amy Heatley who died 28 April 1987
Urn
CARSON

CARSON   limestone - pointed top   No 161 OLD Section

erected by Joseph Carson, Ballyutoag, in memory of this daughter
Jane who departed this life 28 February 1848 aged 26 years also the above
Joseph Carson died 3 June 1849 aged 63 years also his wife
Jane died 18 July 1869 aged 72 years also
James Carson son of Gibson Carson died 20 July 1893 aged 24 years
on map - Gibson and Joseph Carson

CARSON   see Parker   No 162 OLD Section

CARSON   large limestone   No 175 OLD Section

erected by Samuel Carson, Ballyutoague, in memory of his father
John Carson died 14 November 1861 aged 84 years also his mother
Margaret died 28 May 1861 aged 74 years and his brother
James died 8 September 1850 aged 33 years also the said
Samuel Carson died 16 December 1892 aged 75 years
on map - S Carson

CARSON   limestone   No 176 OLD Section

erected by Alexander Carson, Ballyutoague in memory of his beloved daughter
Elizabeth who died 2 August 1868 aged 38 years also his beloved wife
Mary who died 21 September 1874 aged 78 years also the said
Alexander Carson who died 11 January 1878 aged 84 years likewise his
daughter Jane who died 16 January 1888 aged 60 years also his daughter
Mary died 4 September 1908 aged 73 years likewise his son
James who died 27 May 1909 aged 90 years likewise his daughter
Hannah who died 14 December 1912 aged 92 years
on map - Alex Carson

CARSON   grey stone partly sunken   No 177 OLD Section

erected by William Carson of Ballyutoag in memory of his daughter
.... who departed this life 11 ? December 1832 ? aged 11 years
rest of inscription missing

CARUTH   grey granite stone and surround   A-6 Section

CARUTH
in loving memory of
Alexander beloved husband of Madge Caruth died 31 July 1942

CARUTH   black marble stone   A-12 Section

in loving memory of
William died 29 April 1969 and his wife
Meta died 14 March 1970

CARUTH   see Boston   A-13 Section

| CARUTH | black pillar with urn on top | No 028 OLD Section |

erected by Elisha Caruth, Mallusk, in loving memory of his wife
Jane died 18 January 1918 aged 61 years also their sons
Gregory Caruth died 18 January 1896 aged 2 1/2 years
"Pro patria mortin sunt"
Lieut. John Caruth died on wounds received in action in France
10 October 1918 and was interred in British Cemetery at
Tincourt aged 32 years
2nd Lieut. Matthew Caruth who fell at Guinchey, France 9 September 1916
and was interred in Military Cemetery aged 26 years
Elisha Caruth died 29 September 1933 aged 83 years
Right side
in loving memory of Hugh eldest son of Elisha Caruth and
beloved husband of Elizabeth A Caruth died 25 September 1942
Elizabeth A Caruth died 11 April 1970 aged 84 years wife of Hugh Caruth
also their son Hugh died 17 September 1965 aged 40 years
Left side
Arthur Caruth died 13 January 1975
Elizabeth Caruth died 3 October 1990
on map - Elisha Caruth

| CARUTH | see McGready | No 074 OLD Section |

| CARUTH | fallen white marble in surround | No 090A OLD Section |

CARUTH
in loving memory of my dear husband
Hugh F Caruth who died 25 January 1929 aged 83 years also his son
John Stanley Reid who died 23 July 1897 aged 11 years also
Margaret, wife of H F Caruth who died 23 November 1935
Agnes J Caruth who died 19 June 1967
Blessed are the dead who died in the Lord

| CAUGHEY | double grey marble and surround | A-2 Section |

CAUGHEY
in loving memory of David died 28 August 1946 also
his dear wife Florence died 6 December 1982

| CHAMBERS | grey stone in railings | A-11 Section |

CHAMBERS
in loving memory of our dear father
William James Chambers who died 27 October 1930 and our dear mother
Mary Jane Chambers who died 26 June 1933 also their dear son
James who died 7 March 1932 interred in Mount Pleasant, Toronto
and their little grand-daughter
Lyla Moffatt who fell asleep 30 May 1934 aged 3 years and 3 months
Thy will be done

| CHERRY | black granite | A-14 Section |

CHERRY
in loving memory of a dear husband and father
Fred died 9 March 1987

| CHRISTIE | small carved stone | A-4 Section |

erected by John Christie in loving memory of my dearly beloved wife
Jennetta Christie who departed this life on 27 January 1924 aged 60 years

---

| CHRISTIE | see Hamilton | No 136A OLD Section |

| CLARKE | black urn | A-5 Section |

CLARKE   Sarah

| CLARKE | see McGaw | No 042C OLD Section |

| CLYDE | square black marble vase | A-2 Section |

CLYDE

| CLYDE | grey surround | A-8 Section |

CLYDE
in loving memory of my dear husband
James who died 16 June 1962
Peace, perfect peace

| COLGAN | grey stone and surround | A-9 Section |

Elizabeth Colgan died 26 March 1905
George Colgan died 2 March 1906 also my wife
Mary Colgan died 2 June 1938

| COLVIN | see Millar | A-4 Section |

| COLVIN | white marble stone and surround | A-12 Section |

COLVIN
erected to the memory of my mother
Helen McCready died 22 November 1939

| COMPTON | tall stone with carvings | A-10 Section |

erected by William Compton in memory of his dear wife
Minnie Wiseman who departed this life 4 November 1917 aged 32 years
also of her two sisters
Lizzie who departed this life 10 June 1912 aged 22 years
Jeannie who departed this life 21 October 1899 aged 3 years also
Nellie who died 13 November 1918 aged 25 years
Until the day break and the shadows flee away

| COMPTON | white stone and railings | A-11 Section |

in loving memory of our mother
Hessie Compton died 4 August 1914 aged 52 years also our father
Henry died 20 October 1931 aged 73 years also our brother
John died 20 July 1916 aged 26 years interred Stanthorpe, Australia
also our brother Joseph died 20 June 1899 aged 13 months also their
grandchild William died in infancy

| CONNOLLY | large stone and surround | A-4 Section |

The son of God who loved me and gave himself for me.
in loving memory of my dear wife Helen Connolly died 13 May 1926
also our dear daughter Helen died 15 May 1926 also
James Fortescue Connolly dearly loved husband of the above Helen
died 5 November 1964

| CONNOLLY | white marble and surround | A-6 Section |

CONNOLLY
in loving memory of our dear mother
Annie Connolly died 14 June 1959 also our dear brother
John died 25 February 1972 also son-in-law
John Ireland died 8 April 1995
Vase CONNOLLY

| CONNOR | black surround | A-13 Section |

CONNOR
in loving memory of our devoted mother
Elizabeth died 16 February 1979 and her dear son
William died 16 January 1991
At rest
Small vase - in loving memory of grandmother

CONWAY	black marble and surround	A-13 Section

CONWAY
in loving memory of a devoted husband and father
Samuel who died 9 February 1980 also our dear son
Robert died in infancy
Thy will be done

CORNETT	white surround	A-3 Section

CORNETT
in loving memory of my husband
Andrew Cornett J.P. died 5 November 1957 also his wife
Ellen died 10 October 1970 and her son
Robert A McGrath died 7 February 1970

CORNETT	twin granite and surround	A-6 Section

CORNETT
in loving memory of
William loved husband of Henrietta W Cornett died 7 August 1951
also his wife Henrietta W. died 22 June 1978

CORNETT	twin stone and surround	A-6 Section

CORNETT
in loving memory of
Elizabeth Conway Cornett B.A.
born 12 November 1924 died 1 November 1952
also her father John Cornett
born 1 July 1881 died 6 October 1958

CORNETT	see McCammond	A-13 Section

COULTER	small grey marble vase	A-2 Section

COULTER

COURTNEY	black granite stone and surround	A-7 Section

the family burying ground of Robert Courtney

COURTNEY	see Nesbitt	No 143B OLD Section

COWAN	see Johnston	No 061 OLD Section

COWAN	broken cross in railings	No 073A OLD Section

COWAN
Lily S. born 1 December 1915 died 26 October 1916
Maisie born 13 March 1904 died 24 April 1924

COWAN	small grey stone	No 073B OLD Section

COWAN

CRAIG	grey stone and surround	A-2 Section

CRAIG
in loving memory of my dear wife
Annie who died 6 September 1957 also our dear son
Hugh, lost at sea 14 March 1949
The Lord is my shepherd

CRAIG	black headstone	A-5 Section

CRAIG
in loving memory of a devoted husband and father
Ben died 9 October 1979

DEVINE	grey stone and surround	A-11 Section

DEVINE
in loving memory of a devoted husband and father
John Devine died 4 April 1944, his wife and our dear mother
Sarah J. Devine died 4 November 1946, their son and our dear brother
Robert Devine died 11 June 1981

DEVLIN	pink marble stone and surround	A-5 Section

DEVLIN
in loving remembrance of my dear husband
William John Devlin passed away 21 March 1961 also his beloved wife
Anna Mary Devlin passed away 15 March 1982
Right side
children of William John and Anna Mary Devlin
Agnes, William, Robert and Joan Hagan
Died in infancy

DIXON	white stone and railings	A-8 Section

DIXON
in loving memory of my father
William Dixon who died 27 August 1917 also my dear wife
Jennie Dixon who died 30 May 1937 also
William Dixon husband of above who died 18 October 1941 also their daughter
Isabella Brown died 23 December 1970

DOLLAR	see Williamson	No 134 OLD Section

DONALDSON	see Townsley	A-7 Section

DOUGHERTY	white stone in railings	A-11 Section

erected by Robert Dougherty in memory of his dear wife
Jane died December 29 1927 aged 74 and his daughter
Elizabeth died September 29 1902 aged 22 also his daughter
Sarah died March 16 1939 aged 53

DRENNAN	tall white worn stone	A-11 Section

in memory of Samuel G. Drennan beloved husband of Isabella Sharp
who died 15 September 1901
and her daughter Isabella died 16 March 1906
her son Maxwell died 16 April 1907

DUBOIS	see Logan	A-2 Section

DUBOIS	grey stone in metal surround	A-5 Section

DUBOIS
in loving memory of
Sarah Agnes Dubois died 30 June 1948 aged 81 years

DUBOIS	grey marble headstone	A-13 Section

in loving memory of James beloved husband and father
died 21 March 1978 aged 69 years

DUBOYS	see McCallum	A-8 Section

DUFF	see Logan	A-2 Section

ECCLES	marble stone	A-13 Section

in loving memory of my dear husband
David died 29 April 1973
also his devoted wife Mary died 30 May 1996
beloved parents of Carol

EDGAR	black headstone and white surround	A-5 Section

EDGAR
in memory of a loving mother
Mary died 1947 also our dear father
John died 1973
their daughter Sarah died 15 January 1996
dear wife of Hugh Campbell

ELDER	small square white vase	A-5 Section

in loving memory of Hugh Dubois Elder
8 March 1916 to 16 March 1985
to granda - love Gemma and Zara

ELDER	square stone marker	A-8 Section

ELDER
in loving memory

ELLISON	granite & surround	A-1 Section

ELLISON
in loving memory of our dear father
John Smyth who died 22nd November 1943
also my beloved husband James Ellison who died 7th July 1966
also my dear mother Martha Jane Smyth who died 28th August 1977
also her dear daughter Ethel Ellison who died 4th November 1980
At rest

ELLISON	see Major	No 123 OLD Section

FAIRFIELD	see McMillan	A-1 Section

FAIRFIELD	black marble stone	A-6 Section

FAIRFIELD
in loving memory of our dear parents
John died 2 May 1981
Margaret died 7 September 1984 and daughter
Agnes died 24 December 1989

FEARN	white stone	A-2 Section

MEMORIAM
James F Fearn
died 17 January 1944 also his wife
Susan Fearn died 16 September 1957 also their son
Herbert James died 31 March 1960 also their daughter
Mary L Barron died 4 May 1976
At rest
Loving memories of a devoted mother
VASE - Fearn / Barron

FEE	large black surround	A-3 Section

FEE
White Vase - in loving memory

FEE	surround	A-5 Section

FEE
in loving memory of my dear wife
Edith Ingram Fee who died 14 June 1931 also her dear husband
John William Fee died 18 September 1947

FEE	see Parkhill	No 108B OLD Section

FERGUSON — black marble stone and surround — A-2 Section

FERGUSON
in loving memory of our dear parents
Margaret W. died 19 December 1949
Albert died 21 February 1962
also our dear brother
Walter S. died 18 July 1983

FERGUSON — headstone — No 001A OLD Section

erected by Fras. Ferguson, Belfast in memory of his beloved wife
Mary who departed this life 28 May AD 1837 aged 33 years
also his infant child

FERGUSON — slanted worn slate stone — No 046 OLD Section

FERGUSON
.... wife
departed this life 4 February 1808 aged 74 years

FERGUSON — fallen large granite stone — No 145 OLD Section

Thomas Ferguson
in loving memory of his beloved father
William Ferguson of Muckamore
who departed this life 27 September 1864 aged 64 years also his brother
Samuel Ferguson who departed this life 20 September 1876 aged 41 years
and of Mary Ferguson his mother who died 26 November 1886 aged 88 years
likewise his sister Jenny Ferguson who died 10 June 1888 aged 61 years
and his wife Ann Ferguson who died 3 November 1895 aged 74 years
also his sister Agnes Ferguson who died 24 June 1899 aged 68 years
and the beloved Thomas Ferguson died 14 August 1904 aged 78 years
also his sister Sarah Ferguson died 22 November 1913 aged 74 years
Thomas Ferguson, Master Mariner, died 13 May 1923 also his grandson
Thomas Alexander Moore died 6 July 1934
on map - Thomas Ferguson

FERGUSON — broken stone - 7 bits/1 missing — No 146 OLD Section

erected by Ann Ferguson in m......... her dear departed ....
Thomas Ferguson .... December 16 1861
their daughter Barbara died March 23 1824 aged 4 months and their son
John James died August 13 1832 aged 2 years also the said
Ann Ferguson who died February 23 1871 aged 81 years also their daughter
Barbara Ferguson who died June 24 1874 aged 49 years
on map - Mrs Ferguson

FERGUSON	see Wilson	No 147 OLD Section

FINCH — black marble stone and surround — A-3 Section

FINCH
in loving memory of my dear wife
Margaret died 27 August 1961 also her husband
Sandy died 7 September 1966

FINLAY — black marble — A-1 Section

in loving memory of our dear parents
James 1907 - 1961
Sadie 1908 - 1995
also
Agnes and James died in infancy

FINLAY — small stone in railings — A-4 Section

in loving memory of Andrew Finlay died 15 July 1930 also his wife
Susan died 14 January 1937 also her sister
Jane Allen died 18 September 1938

FINLAY	triple plot in railings	A-4 Section

erected by James Finlay in remembrance of his daughter
Margaret C Finlay died 3 December 1933
Black Urn   BASKIN

FINLAY	see Alexander	A-11 Section

FINLAY	no stone	No 171 OLD Section

on map - Jas Finlay

FINLAY	white marble stone with carving	No 172 OLD Section

erected by Allen Finlay, Hydepark in loving memory of his wife
Margaret who died 11 October 1892 aged 30 years also the above named
Allen Finlay who died 9 January 1936 aged 73 years
on map - Charlotte Finlay

FINLAY	stone and railings	No 173 OLD Section

erected by William Finlay of Hydepark
in affectionate remembrance of his son
William John who died 23 April 1871 aged 6 years also the said
William Finlay who died 18 December 1876 aged 49 years also his wife
Jane who died 11 February 1918 aged 90 years also Charlotte
beloved wife of Alexander Finlay who died 20 October 1924 aged 57 years
also the above named Alexander Finlay who died 13 August 1944 aged 77 yrs
also Charlotte Reid (Lottie) daughter of the above named Alexander and
Charlotte Finlay who died 19 April 1993 aged 91 years
on map - Charlotte Finlay

FINNEY	grey marble stone and surround	A-2 Section

FINNEY
Jeannie Agnew passed from death unto life 2 February 1966
also her husband William died 9 November 1978
also their devoted daughter
Margaret McA Dalglish died 27 August 1985

FINNEY	see Williamson	No 134 OLD Section

FLACK	curved sandstone headstone	No 052 OLD Section

erected by a few of his brother apprentices in memory of
James Flack, shipwright of Belfast
who departed this life 31 October 1844 aged 25 years
"Though his dust to dusts returned
Yet his name we'll mention oft
For through life his God he loved
And now his soul is gone aloft"
on map - Jas Hollywood

FLEMING	double white marble and surround	A-2 Section

in loving memory of my dear wife and our beloved mother
Agnes May Moore Fleming who died 22 December 1957 also our dear father
William Fleming who died 4 June 1978 also their grandson
Baby Fleming died April 1968

FLETCHER	no stone	No 051 OLD Section

on map - Wm Fletcher

FORSYTHE	black granite stone and surround	A-9 Section

FORSYTHE
in affectionate remembrance of
James departed this life 17 November 1985
devoted husband of Sadie

| FOSTER | see McKeown | A-1 Section |

| FOSTER | no stone | No 018 OLD Section |

on map - Foster

| FRAZER | grey marble and surround | A-13 Section |

FRAZER
in loving memory of May who died 26 April 1972
dear wife of Robert John Frazer MBE who died 15 April 1978

| FULLERTON | black stone | A-3 Section |

FULLERTON
in loving memory of a dear wife and mother
May nee Smyth died 27 January 1970 aged 66 years

| FULLERTON | see Millar | A-5 Section |

| FULTON | see Bigger | A-13 Section |

| GAILEY | grey granite stone | A-5 Section |

in memory of Ethel Gailey died 7 September 1947
beloved wife of James Gailey died 3 May 1972

| GAMBLE | grey marble stone and surround | A-2 Section |

GAMBLE
in loving memory of William K Gamble died 1 Jamuary 1961
also Esther Logan died 4 January 1941 also
Margaret F Gamble died 20 May 1967

| GARRET | tall granite stone | No 100A OLD Section |

here lieth the body of Martha Garret wife to James Garret
of the Lodge parish of Saintfield in the County of Down
who died 1 July 1811 also the body of the above named
James Garret who departed this life 12 March 1832 aged 79 years
on map - Chas B Smith

| GAULT | black marble stone with surround | A-14 Section |

GAULT
in loving memory of our beloved mother and grandmother
Mary Agnes died 15 September 1996
2 black urns - Mother

| GEDDIS | grey stone | A-4 Section |

GEDDIS
in loving memory of a devoted wife and mother
Harriet died 20 August 1974 also a beloved husband and father
Lamond died 19 February 1992
Till we meet

| GEDDIS | black marble stone | A-9 Section |

GEDDIS
in loving memory of a dear wife and mother
Frances Louise (Lulu) died 1 April 1976
The Lord is my shepherd

GEORGE	stone and surround	A-1 Section

erected by Mary Jane George
in loving memory of her dear husband
James George of Hydepark who fell asleep 13th July 1926
also the above named Mary Jane George who fell asleep 5th January 1929
"Until He Come"
GEORGE

GEORGE	grey marble stone and surround	A-3 Section

GEORGE
in loving memory of
Samuel beloved husband of Mildred George died 24 January 1958

GEORGE	stone in surround	No 005B OLD Section

The family burying ground of Samuel George

GEORGE	see Bigger	No 005C OLD Section

GEORGE	Iron memorial and surround	No 167 OLD Section

The burying place of Samuel George
Mallusk 1881
on map - S George

GIFFIN	see Russell	No 121 OLD Section

GILLESPIE	black marble headstone	A-6 Section

GILLESPIE
in loving memory of our dear parents
William died 8 February 1959
Elizabeth died 4 October 1972
their daughter
Sarah (Sadie) died 7 April 1983

GILLESPIE	grey stone with surround	A-10 Section

in loving memory of a dear wife and devoted mother
Agnes Jane died 21 October 1965 also her dear husband
John died 20 December 1970
Ours to remember

GILLESPIE	see Millar	A-11 Section

GILMORE	stone and surround	A-1 Section

in loving memory of
William Gilmore of Carnanee who died 10th August 1894 aged 62 years
interred in Ballylinney and his wife
Mary Harper who died 11th February 1936 aged 92 years also their daughters
Agnes Turvill who died 4th July 1920 aged 45 years
interred in Vancouver B.C
Left Edging
Ellen Quern died 8th November 1887 aged 4 years
Right Edging
Susanna died 26th November 1887 aged 10 years

GILMORE	see Nelson	A-8 Section

GILMORE	black marble urn on pedestal	A-8 Section

in memory of James Gilmore died 8 December 1961

| GLASS | grey stone and iron surround | A-6 Section |

GLASS
in loving memory of Sarah Glass died 22 November 1959 also
James Goodwin died 23 June 1963 also his wife
Sarah Agnes died 24 August 1963

| GLASS | tall stone with railings | No 106 OLD Section |

erected by Joseph Glass, Cottonmount, in memory of his father
Thomas Glass who died January 31 1867 aged 73 years also his mother
Sarah who died April 23 1882 aged 82 years, his wife
Susanna Glass died 28 January 1908 aged 70 years, his daughter
Janet Patterson died 8 June 1915 aged 37 years also the said
Joseph Glass died 15 February 1919 aged 83 years also
Frank Patterson died 15 March 1970 aged 68 years also his wife
Annie Patterson died 5 November 1975 aged 72 years, their daughter
Roberta (Ruby) died 26 November 1987 aged 61 years
Black vase
Patterson
on map - Frank Patterson

| GOODWIN | see Glass | A-6 Section |

| GORDON | white stone and railings | A-11 Section |

Until the day break
erected by
Sarah Blair and Alice Curran
to the memory of their father
Thomas Gordon who died 31 October 1864, their brothers and sisters
Alice and Thomas who died in infancy
Martha Jane who died 26 March 1872 aged 7
Thomas James who died 11 April 1872 aged 9
John who died 5 November 1887 aged 37
all interred in Donegore
Samuel who died 19 December 1899 aged 46 and their mother
Sarah Gordon who died 2 August 1904 aged 78 years also
Samuel Gordon dearly beloved and devoted son of Francis and Sarah Blair
who died 12 September 1913 aged 27
Samuel G. Blair died 1913
Sarah Blair died 1940
John Gordon Blair died 1960
Evelyn Maria Blair died 1984

| GORDON | see Parker | No 070 OLD Section |

| GOURLEY | black marble stone and surround | A-6 Section |

in loving memory of my dear mother
Susan Mulvenna died 3 May 1975 aged 75 years also my dear father
James Gourley of Shane's Hill, Craigarogan died 26 February 1945 aged 76
also my dear aunt Janet Kane died 19 January 1961 aged 85
Ours to remember

| GRAHAM | granite stone and surround | A-3 Section |

GRAHAM
in loving memory of
William Harkness loved husband of Sadie Graham who died 27 April 1953
also his dear wife Sadie who died 22 February 1980
At rest

| GRAHAM | see Taylor | A-6 Section |

| GRAHAM | granite stone in surround | No 021 OLD Section |

GRAHAM
on map - Mrs Graham

| GRAHAM | large black marble with railings | No 159 OLD Section |

GRAHAM
whose names are written in the book of life
on map - Graham

| GRANGE | see McBride | A-1 Section |

| GRANT | metal shield | No 113 OLD Section |

the family burying ground of
Patrick Grant
1830

| GRAY | see Nimmons | A-7 Section |

| GREEN | no stone | No 026 OLD Section |

on map - James Green, J Hamilton, T Williamson

| GREENLEES | granite stone and surround | A-3 Section |

in loving memory of our dear daughter
Sarah Robina (Ruby) died 29 May 1947 aged 26 years also her mother
Sarah Jane Greenlees died 1 January 1950 also her father
Edward Greenlees died 3 October 1953
In His presence is fulness of joy.
GREENLEES

| GREENSPON | black marble and surround | A-13 Section |

in loving memory of my dear mother Matilda died 7 February 1976
also her dear son Joseph beloved husband of Olive died 29 March 1982
Shalom
At Rest

| GREENWOOD | see Hunter | A-8 Section |

| GREENWOOD | no stone | No 004 OLD Section |

on map - Margaret Greenwood

| GREER | capped limestone headstone | No 109 OLD Section |

erected by George Greer of Hightown in memory of his father
Robert Greer who died 16 May 1856 aged 82 years also his son
John who died 3 March 1867 aged 19 years also his son
Robert who died 22 March 1875 aged 32 years
The said George Greer who died 16 March 1880 aged 81 years also his son
William Greer who died 16 July 1898 aged 60 years also his wife
Eliza Greer who died 20 April 1899 aged 89 years also his son
Joseph Greer who died 23 June 1925 aged 81 years
and was interred in Enniskillen also his daughter
Eliza Jane who died 22 May 1931 in her 86th year
on map - John Greer

| GREER | white marble stone | No 163 OLD Section |

the burying ground of Robert J Greer
Ballycraigy
on map - R J Greer

| GUTHRIE | black marble stone | A-2 Section |

GUTHRIE
in loving memory of my dear husband John died 12 January 1980
a beloved wife and mother Elizabeth died 13 April 1994
Ever in our thoughts

HARPER	see Gilmore	A-1 Section

HARPER	black marble vase	A-2 Section

HARPER

HARVEY	large worn fallen stone	No 128A OLD Section

the burying place of Samuel Harvey, Belfast 1877
in loving memory of my dear husband Samuel Harvey
who died 28 September 1906 aged 80 years
his last words were
I Know that my Redeemer liveth
Agnes Harvey
In memory of the above Agnes Harvey
for 54 years the faithful wife of the said Samuel Harvey
she died 7 June 1908
Trusting in the atoning .... of Jesus
on map - Harvey

HARVEY	large worn fallen stone	No 128B OLD Section

erected by Hannah Harvey
in loving memory of her beloved husband
William Harvey who departed this life 13 February 186. aged 65 years
May his children tread the steps he trod
Till death, earths ties shall sever
and now loved husband, friend, farewell
Farewell, but not forever
Hannah Harvey
died 18 May 1867 aged 73 years
Hannah Jane
died 18 March 1866 aged 27 ? years
Blessed are the dead ....

HAWORTH	see Hunter	A-8 Section

HAWTHORNE	see Ross	A-10 Section

HAYES	no stone	No 114 OLD Section

on map - Ben and Wm Hayes

HEATLEY	see Carson	A-13 Section

HENDERSON	grey marble stone	A-5 Section

HENDERSON
in loving memory of our parents
Kathleen died 21 August 1952
William 17 June 1970 also our brother
Andrew Alexander 8 April 1983
Worthy of remembrance

HENDERSON	black marble stone	A-6 Section

HENDERSON
in loving memory of Isobel died 6 May 1992
Loved and remembered always

HERIVEL	granite stone and surround	A-3 Section

HERIVEL
in memory of John Jamieson
beloved husband of Josephine Allison Herivel and son of
John William Herivel of Alderney, Channel Islands died 12 May 1951
and his wife Josephine Allison Herivel nee Moat
died 19 May 1974 in her 88th year

| HERRON | white marble stone and surround | A-6 Section |

HERRON
in loving memory of Jane who died 2 October 1949
beloved wife of John Herron who died 6 May 1969
Mary A. died 26 April 1975 their daughter and wife of John Kennedy
In His presence is fulness and joy

| HETHERINGTON | grey marble and surround | A-2 Section |

HETHERINGTON
in loving memory of Joseph who fell asleep 28 December 1939
He was not for God took him
also his beloved wife Mary who followed on 11 May 1980

| HEWITT | grey marble | A-13 Section |

HEWITT
in loving memory of my dear wife and our devoted mother
Wilhelmina who died 29 January 1985
Till we meet

| HIGGINSON | grey marble headstone | A-13 Section |

HIGGINSON
treasured memories of
John dear husband and father died 23 April 1989
How great Thou art

| HIGGINSON | black marble stone | A-14 Section |

HIGGINSON
precious memories of our dear mother
Mary Ellen (May) died 28 June 1994

| HOEY | see Devers | A-13 Section |

| HOLLYWOOD | see Flack | No 052 OLD Section |

| HOLLYWOOD | no stone | No 055 OLD Section |

on map - Mary Hollywood

| HOPE | grey stone and surround | A-2 Section |

HOPE
in loving memory of my dear mother
Mary Jane died 15 February 1952 also my dear father
Alexander died 31 March 1959 and his son
George Hope died 9 January 1972

| HOPE | see Moat | No 027 OLD Section |

| HOPE | sandstone upright square memorial | No 049 OLD Section |

to the memory of Luke M Hope (Editor of the Rushlight)
whose life was distinguished by the superiority of his talents, the purity
of his principles and the simplicity of his manners.
This monument is placed by a few of the many friends who valued his worth
and regret his premature death.
The tear that we shed through in secret it rolls
Shall long keep his memory green in our souls
Left Side born 25.6.1794
Right Side died 5.12.1827
on map - McNeilly Hope

HOPE   large limestone memorial   No 050 OLD Section
                         sacred to the memory of
                James Hope who was born in 1764 and died 1847
         One of nature's noblest works, an honest man. Steadfast in faith and
      always hopeful in the divine protection. In the best era of his country's
         history a soldier in her cause: and in the worst of times still
      faithful to it: ever true to himself, and to those who trusted in him
         he remained to the last unchanged and unchangeable in his fidelity.
         also his wife Rose Mullan born 3 December 1770 died 25 May 1830
                              also his sons
              Robert Emmet Hope born April 1812 died 23 May 1864
           Henry Joy McCracken Hope born 1809 died 19 January 1872
               his father and mother John Hope and Sarah Speers
               Oval stone relief engraving of Irish wolfhound

HOPE   small grey stone   No 050A OLD Section

                   here lieth at rest MacNeilly Hope
             grandson of James Hope and the last of his stock
                  born 6 December 1843 died 8 April 1920
              Mary Eliza Hope born 22 May 1864 died 16 June 1929
             Thomas Templeton born 7 February 1883 died 19 May 1903
               Margaret born 17 June 1886 died 12 April 1918
                      No go néirchidh an la

HORNER   grey stone and surround   A-2 Section

                                 HORNER
               in loving memory of a dear husband and father
                   Robert James Horner died 10 July 1962
                   his wife Margaret Horner died 21 July 1977
                            Always remembered

HORNER   black stone white surround   A-4 Section

                                 HORNER
         in loving memory of Agnes Horner died 1925 and baby James died 1945
                         son of James and Winnie

HORNER   tall - carved top   No 126 OLD Section

             erected by Mary Horner in memory of her beloved husband
          William Horner who died 8 July 1880 aged 46 years also their daughter
        Margaret who died 13 August 1875 aged 2 yrs and 9 months also his daughter
                  Jane who died 19 July 1881 AE 21 years also the above
                Mary Horner who died 28 December 1917 aged 82 years
             Robert Horner died 25 October 1905 aged 53 years, his wife
              Emily Horner died 7 May 1911 aged 56 years also their son
               John Horner died 2 September 1943 aged 65 years
                      on map - John and Mary Horner

HOSICK   white marble stone and surround   A-3 Section

                            in loving memory of
                Alfred Hosick died 29 November 1950 aged 79 years also his wife
         Mary Ann Hosick died 5 February 1956 aged 82 years also their son-in-law
                John J Taggart died 1 December 1974 aged 80 years and his wife
                 Sarah Taggart died 17 March 1983 aged 87 years

HOUSTON   small red plaque   A-3 Section

                                HOUSTON
                             Adam and Mary
                  placed by their grandchildren in Canada

HOUSTON   iron surround   A-5 Section

                   in loving memory of my dear husband
             James Houston died 19 November 1936 also our dear mother
                   Eleanor Houston died 5 November 1945

HOUSTON   no stone   No 088 OLD Section

                        on map - Wm A. Houston

HOUSTON	metal shield	No 112 OLD Section

the family burying ground of
Alexander Houston
1830
on map - Houston

HOY	small stone in surround	No 020 OLD Section

the burial place of W J Hoy
on map - Wm Hoy

HUGHES	black marble and surround	A-2 Section

HUGHES
in loving memory of my dearly beloved husband
James Hughes died 18 March 1940
For I know that my Redeemer liveth

HUGHES	see Logan	A-2 Section

HUGHES	grey granite stone and surround	A-3 Section

HUGHES
in loving memory of Robert died 11 June 1963
also his beloved wife Jean died 20 June 1993

HULL	see McMillen	A-8 Section

HUME	grey stone	A-13 Section

HUME
in loving memory of our dear son
George Morrison Hume died 18 January 1975 aged 18 years

HUNTER	vase	A-3 Section

HUNTER

HUNTER	iron surround	A-5 Section

HUNTER
in remembrance of dear Alex
who was called from this life on the 10 June 1933 in his 14th year

HUNTER	see Nimmons	A-7 Section

HUNTER	granite obelisk and urn	A-8 Section

erected by Joseph Hunter in loving memory of his dear wife
Annie Haworth born June 1842 died 18 March 1914 also his youngest son
Herbert James born May 1884 died 22 January 1914 also his grandson
Joseph Hunter born July 1907 died 24 April 1908 also his granddaughter
Gertrude Hunter Greenwood died 20 July 1920 aged 4 months also the
above named Joseph Hunter died 28 November 1922 aged 80 years
HUNTER
Vase
GREENWOOD
George Edward Greenwood son-in-law died 2 July 1941 also
Annie wife of the above named died 5 January 1969
Peace, perfect peace
GREENWOOD

HUNTER	no stone	No 010 OLD Section

on map - John Hunter

HUNTER	grey stone and railings	No 090 OLD Section

HUNTER
Andrew Hunter died 16 July 1934 aged 62
He fought a good fight and kept the faith.

HUTCHINSON	granite headstone and surround	A-6 Section

HUTCHINSON
in loving memory of Thomas
beloved husband of Janie Hutchinson
who died 15 June 1947 also the above
Janie died 13 March 1973

IRELAND	see Connolly	A-6 Section

IRELAND	see Scroggie	No 002 OLD Section

IRVINE	grey marble stone	A-2 Section

IRVINE
Isaac Alexander
4 May 1932 - 18 February 1996
beloved husband of Bertha
loved and respected father of Graeme, Linda and Julie-Anne
In death as in life, a quiet man.

IRVINE	marble stone and surround	A-6 Section

IRVINE
in loving memory of a devoted mother
Annie died 19 November 1970 also her dear son
Robert died 19 September 1979
Always in our thoughts

IRVINE	no stone	No 170 OLD Section

on map - Andrew Irvine

IRWIN	see McMeekin	A-8 Section

JACKSON	grey marble stone and vase	A-6 Section

JACKSON
in loving memory of
Gordon a dear husband and devoted father died 16 November 1981
Till we meet again
Vase
JACKSON
Samuel died 4.8.79
Mary died 25.2.89

JACKSON	black urn	No 129A OLD Section

JACKSON

JAMISON	no stone	No 023 OLD Section

on map - T Jamison

JELLIE	fallen limestone	No 153 OLD Section

erected by Sarah Jellie of Kingsmoss in memory of her husband
William Jellie who died 17 ..... 1855 aged 60 years also of her son
Alexander Jellie who died 13 .... 1847 aged 20 years also the above
Mrs Sarah Jellie who died 15 April 1879 aged 80 years
"Rest in peace"

JENKINS	white surround	A-1 Section
	JENKINS	

JOHNSTON	see Martin	A-2 Section

JOHNSTON	stone in iron railings	A-5 Section

in loving memory of William Henry
beloved husband of Isabella Johnston called home 12 January 1951
also his son John died 21 August 1951 interred in Rockhampton, Australia
also the above Isabella Johnston called home 10 October 1957
Safe in God's keeping

JOHNSTON	wooden cross in white railings	A-5 Section

Thomas Johnston 1922 - 1988

JOHNSTON	no stone	No 032 OLD Section

on map - Finlay Johnston

JOHNSTON	granite stone	No 061 OLD Section

in memory of John Johnston of Whiteabbey
who departed this life 30 Nov 1864 aged 84 years also his father
Hugh Johnston who died December 1794 aged 56 years also his mother
Janet Rea who died January 1824 aged 86 years also of their son
Samuel Johnston who died in London 6 March 1816 aged 46 years and
Thomas Johnston who died at Whiteabbey November 1832 aged 55 yrs also
their daughter Alice who died March 1829 aged 55 years
on map - Cowan

JOHNSTONE	see Logan	A-2 Section

JONES	see Nesbitt	No 143B OLD Section

JUNK	black granite - heart shaped	A-13 Section

JUNK
in loving memory of my darling mother
Mary McCullough died 8 December 1992 aged 83 years
In God's keeping
Memorial Urn
Mary McCullough 8.12.92

KANE	granite stone	A-6 Section

KANE
Redeemed

KANE	see Gourley	A-6 Section

KANE	black metal shield	No 075 OLD Section

burying ground of David Kane, Belfast

KANE   black granite in surround   No 077 OLD Section

erected by David and Lizzie Kane in affectionate rembrance of
their father Samuel Kane who departed this life 31 May 1896 and
their mother Eliza Kane who departed this life 19 July 1893
also their brothers
Samuel died 19 April 1895
James died 24 February 1929
also their sisters
Maggie died 22 December 1866
Agnes died 25 September 1912
Martha died 15 August 1930
Mary died 13 August 1939
and a sister died in infancy
and on sides
also David died 8 April 1943 also
Lizzie Kane died 26 December 1848
on map - Kane

KELL   large granite stone and surround   A-11 Section

KELL
erected by Isabel D. Kell
in loving memory of her dear husband
William Kell who died 2 March 1921 and the above
Isabel D. Kell who died 25 March 1939
Right side
in memory of Sarah Murdock died 5 December 1901 aged 70 years

---

KELL   black pillar (urn, base & surround)   No 034 OLD Section

erected by Jane Kell, Trench, in memory of her husband
Joseph Kell who died 26 March 1867 aged 68 years also two of their children
who died in infancy also their daughter
Ellen who died 10 December 1901 aged 42 years also the above named
Jane Kell who died 13 August 1905 aged 80 years also their son
Joseph who died 24 May 1913 aged 58 years also
Left side
Jane Kell wife of Joseph who died 24 May 1934 and her son
Joseph who died 19 July 1971 also Elsie Kell, J.P. wife of Joseph
who died 13 April 1988 aged 90 years
on map - Mrs Kell

KELSO   stone and surround   A-2 Section

KELSO
in loving memory of Frances dearly loved and devoted wife of
John Kelso entered into rest 7 January 1942 also the above
John Kelso entered into rest 7 April 1943

KELSO   grey stone and surround   A-2 Section

KELSO
erected by Robert Kelso in loving memory of my dear father
William John died 29 September 1943 aged 82 years also my dear mother
Margaret died 25 February 1953 aged 88 years

KELSO   cream washed stone and surround   No 009 OLD Section

erected by Elizabeth Kelso in memory of her beloved husband
David Kelso late of Kilcreel who died 7 November 1888 aged 81 years
also the above named Elizabeth Kelso who died 6 April 1894 aged 72 years
Agnes Webb who died 9 February 1903 aged 7 1/2 years
James Kane Webb who died 17 April 1903 aged 4 months
also Meta the darling daughter of George and Meta Webb, Ballyhenry
who died 20 January 1934 aged 15 months
Mary Webb who died 2 January 1937
also her husband Charles Webb who died 24 March 1950

KELSO	small fallen sandstone	No 024 OLD Section

KELSO
here
lieth the body of Andrew Kelso of Windyhill
who departed this life the 1 January 1798 aged 84 years also
Arabella Kelso his wife who departed this life January 26 1800 aged 75 yrs
here lieth also the body of their son
Joseph Kelso of Gowlen-ward
who departed this life the 12 December 1799 aged 33 years
also here lieth the body of Susanna Kelso wife of Joseph Kelso
also of Gowlen-ward who died ..... 11th 1802 aged 27 years
on map - Chas Watt

KELSO	black marble stone and surround	No 081 OLD Section

KELSO
the family burying ground of the late Samuel and Ellen Kelso
late of Ballyhenry and Lyle Hill
Worthy of everlasting remembrance
on map - John Kelso

KELSO	tall limestone headstone	No 130 OLD Section

sacred to the memory of Alexr. Kelso of Hydepark
born 1806 died 1857 also his wife
Eliza Jane Kelso born 1826 died 1884
"Prepare to meet thy God"
on map - Wm Kelso

KEMPSTON	see Thompson	No 044 OLD Section

KENNEDY	see Herron	A-6 Section

KENNEDY	no stone	No 131A OLD Section

on map - Kennedy

KENNEDY	no stone	No 133 OLD Section

on map - Kennedy

KENNEDY	see Speer	No 140A OLD Section

KENYON	double black marble & surround	A-1 Section

KENYON
in loving memory of Mary Agnes Kenyon
who died 20th January 1929 aged 62 years
also her husband James Kenyon who died 1st March 1912 aged 43 years and
was interred in Stockport Borough Cemetery
Right surround
their son James Wright died 7 January 1960

KERR	stone and surround	A-7 Section

KERR
in loving memory
The Lord's my shepherd

KERR	surround	A-11 Section

KERR - BOAL

KIRK	black vase	A-9 Section

KIRK

| KIRKPATRICK | granite stone and surround | A-5 Section |

KIRKPATRICK

| KIRKPATRICK | grey marble headstone | A-13 Section |

KIRKPATRICK
in loving memory of my dear wife
Mina who died 7 June 1983 also her dear husband
Victor who died 29 November 1986

| KIRKWOOD | see Williamson | No 134 OLD Section |

| KNOX | black marble and surround | A-2 Section |

KNOX
in loving memory of a devoted husband and father
George Knox who died 13 April 1960 also a beloved wife and mother
Mary who died 11 February 1990

| LEE | stone and surround | A-5 Section |

LEE
in loving memory of my dear wife
Mary who died 13 September 1956 aged 54 years also her dear husband
Edward died 8 June 1963 aged 68 years

| LEEBURN | grey marble stone | A-13 Section |

LEEBURN
in loving memory of a devoted husband and father
William John who died 7 September 1975 also a dear wife and mother
Margaret Ann who died 7 February 1995
Till we meet

| LEEBURN | white urn | No 025A OLD Section |

E E Leeburn died 5 February 1955
on map - William C Leeburn

| LEIGHBURN | grey stone and railings | A-8 Section |

LEIGHBURN
in loving memory of our dear brother
Alexander who died 24 June 1935
also mother who died 16 September 1927
father who died 28 January 1928
interred in Old Ground

| LEIGHBURN | black iron shield | No 025B OLD Section |

the Leighburn family burying ground 1894

| LEWIS | white marble stone and surround | A-6 Section |

erected in loving memory of our dear mother
Mary Lewis, Ballysillan, died 16 May 1942 also
Evelyn Victoria McCallan daughter of the above and
loved wife of William McCallan died 1 May 1981
At rest

| LEWIS | see Watt | A-8 Section |

| LINDSAY | see Bigger | No 015A OLD Section |

LOCKHART	grey stone on cement base	No 084 OLD Section

erected by James Lockhart in memory of his beloved wife
Isabella who died 12 February 1876 aged 28 years also his daughter
Mary Ann who died 17 August 1860 aged 14 months also his son
Robert who died 25 May 1901 aged 22 years
Asleep in Jesus
on map - F W Lockhart
n.b dates are correct - must have been married twice

LOCKHART	limestone - curved top	No 157 OLD Section

erected by Isaac Lockhart in memory of his beloved wife
Margaret who died 20 March 1868 aged 21 years
on map - Lockhart

LOGAN	square black vase	A-2 Section

Evangeline Logan died 5 February 1995 aged 81 years

LOGAN	double white stone and surround	A-2 Section

LOGAN
in loving memory of a devoted wife and mother
Eleanor Hughes (Ellie) who died 19 June 1976
also her beloved husband and loving father
William John who died 28 December 1988
Redeemed
Black Vase
DUFF
James R died 16 June 1954
The Lord is my shepherd
also his wife Anne died 25 November 1977
Black Vase
JOHNSTONE
William died 15 July 1961 At rest
Annie died 14 May 1978
William Jnr died 7 August 1971

LOGAN	see Officer	A-2 Section

LOGAN	grey marble and surround	A-2 Section

LOGAN
in loving memory of Elizabeth Dubois died 30 September 1967
Erected by her daughter and son-in-law

LOGAN	see Gamble	A-2 Section

LOGAN	black marble stone	A-5 Section

LOGAN
treasured memories of a dear husband and devoted father
Thomas who died 7 June 1985
Resting where no shadows fall

LOONEY	see McNeice	A-10 Section

LOUGH	stone and surround	A-5 Section

LOUGH
in loving memory of my dear parents
Samuel died 25 July 1952
Mary died 22 July 1974 also my sister
Mary Jane died 22 October 1974

LOUGHLIN	small broken fallen stone	No 179 OLD Section

erected by Jas M Loughlin, Carnmoney
in loving memory of his father
John M Loughlin who departed this life 7 June 1850 aged 60 years

LUNEY	grey stone	A-5 Section

in loving memory of
Mary E D Luney who died 24 October 1946 aged 47 years

LUNEY	headstone	No 001 OLD Section

erected by Martha Luney in memory of her father
Manassah Luney who died 23 May 1838 aged 60 years also her brother
Patrick Luney who died 7 September 1844 aged 27 years also her mother
Letitia Luney who died 24 October 1868 aged 83 years
on Map - Matthew Luney and James Magee

LYLE	stone and surround	A-1 Section

erected by Mary Lyle
in loving memory of her dear husband
Robert Lyle, Ruthvale died 6th December 1927
also the above Mary Lyle died 30th June 1935

LYLE	grey marble stone and surround	A-3 Section

LYLE
in loving memory of
William beloved husband of Letitia Lyle died 20 May 1961
Jeannie R Lyle died 11 February 1970 wife of James Lyle died 7 June 1974

LYLE	obliterated sunken stone	No 137 OLD Section

on map - Samuel Lyle

LYNAS	long low granite stone	A-9 Section

LYNAS

LYNESS	black marble stone	A-13 Section

LYNESS
in loving memory of my wife and our dear mother
Harriett died 15 April 1975

MacAULEY	see Alexander	No 058 OLD Section

MAGEE	square stone vase	A-5 Section

MAGEE

MAGEE	see Luney	No 001 OLD Section

MAGEE	metal shield and railings	No 007 OLD Section

the family burying ground of Thomas Magee
on map - Thomas Magee

MAGEE	small stone and railings	No 138 OLD Section

the family burying ground of James Magee
on map - Jas A Magee

MAJOR	small worn stone	No 123 OLD Section

this stone was erected by Thomas Major
in memory of his father and mother
his father died March 21 1755 aged 36 years
his mother died September 24 .. ? aged 42 years
also 4 of Thomas's children viz
John, Martha, Thomas and Jenner
on map - Tom Ellison

MARCUS	grey stone	A-13 Section

MARCUS
in loving memory of a devoted husband and father
George Sheridan died 22 October 1980

MARKS	white stone and surround	A-3 Section

MARKS
in loving memory of my beloved husband and our dear father
Joseph Marks died 5 June 1960 also his beloved wife and our dear mother
Isabella died 23 February 1962
Always remembered. Gone to be with Christ.

MARTIN	marble stone and surround	A-2 Section

MARTIN
in loving memory of a devoted husband and father
Robert Alexander died 13 March 1989 beloved husband of Elizabeth
also his father-in-law Hugh Samuel Johnston died 20 December 1988
beloved husband of Violet
The Lord is my shepherd
Left surround
Violet Wright died 3 February 1940
her husband William Wright died 24 July 1952
Right surround
Elizabeth Boyd died 5 February 1940
her mother Elizabeth Boyd died 13 July 1974

MASON	grey stone and surround	A-2 Section

MASON
in loving memory of Georgina beloved wife of Norman G Mason
who died 1 March 1957 also her beloved husband
Norman G Mason who died 23 September 1958
Black vase MASON
also Conifer Tree planted in grave

MASSEY	black marble and surround	A-14 Section

MASSEY
in loving memory of my dear wife
Anna Isobella died 29 April 1987
also her beloved husband William died 14 July 1994
Loved and remembered

MATCHETT	grey stone and surround	A-7 Section

MATCHETT
in loving memory of my dear wife
Sarah Matchett died 14 January 1947 also her dear husband
William John died 22 March 1966 also their beloved daughter-in-law
Meta died 14 January 1971
Black vase MATCHETT

MATHER	iron disc	A-8 Section

the family burying ground of
R. Mather 1919

MAWHINNEY	black stone & surround	A-1 Section

MAWHINNEY
in loving memory of our dear parents
James died 23rd October 1971
Martha died 7th December 1976
Always in our thoughts

MAWHINNEY	stone and surround	A-2 Section

erected by Sarah Mawhinney in loving memory of her husband
Samuel Mawhinney who died 7 June 1940 also the above
Sarah Mawhinney died 12 March 1945
Jesus only, crown Him Lord of all

MAWHINNEY	see Anderson	A-5 Section

MAYNES	black urn	A-11 Section

MAYNES

McALISTER	tall sandstone behind tree	No 072 OLD Section

erected by Alexr. McAlister, Ballycraigy, in memory of his father
John McAlister who departed this life 7 May 1872 ae 75 years and of his
brother John who died 3 June 1866 ae 33 years also of his sister
Sarah who died 22 August 1869 ae 40 years and of his son
John who died 19 March 1869 ae 11 months also his mother
Margaret who died 11 March 1886 aged 88 years also his wife
Agnes McCarrol died 25 July 1893 aged 54 years also their son
James died 15 August 1895 aged 30 years also their youngest son
Robert died 19 November 1897 aged 16 years also the erector
who died 2 November 1903 aged 70 years
on map - Alan McAllister

McBIRNEY	see Carson	A-8 Section

MCBRIDE	tall carved white marble & surround	A-1 Section

McBride
in loving memory of a devoted husband and father
James McBride died 23rd March 1966
also his dear wife Adeline nee Grange died 12 October 1995

McBURNEY	black granite stone	A-11 Section

McBURNEY
in loving memory of our dear parents
John died 31 August 1951
Jeannie died 8 June 1989
At rest

McCALLAN	see Lewis	A-6 Section

McCALLUM	headstone	A-8 Section

in loving memory of Samuel McCallum of Kings Moss
who departed this life on 7 April 1909 also his beloved daughter
Maggie Duboys who departed this life on 21 October 1919 also my daughter
Mary Wylie died 20 June 1921 interred in Woodland Cemetery, Chicago

McCAMMOND	white stone and surround	A-4 Section

McCAMMOND
in loving memory of William died 29 May 1926 also his daughter-in-law
Agnes died 30 August 1932 also his son
James died 19 November 1980 aged 84 years also his daughter-in-law
Joanna died 27 August 1990 aged 83 years
At rest

McCAMMOND	grey marble stone	A-5 Section

McCAMMOND
in loving memory of Edith nee Rhodes who died 18 April 1943 and her
husband Francis (Frank) who died 30 March 1965

McCAMMOND	grey stone, vase and surround	A-8 Section

McCAMMOND

McCAMMOND	black stone	A-13 Section

McCAMMOND
in loving memory of Sgt. William Henry McCammond R.A.F.V.R
killed in action 15 December 1942 aged 26 years
also his brother-in-law John A Cornett
who died 29 September 1984 aged 66 years

McCANN	white marble stone in railings	No 071 OLD Section

McCANN
in loving memory of Hildegard H W died 29 April 1963 aged 66 years
also her husband Albert V died 16 November 1972 aged 75 years
on map - Mrs McCann

McCARROL	see McAlister	No 072 OLD Section

McCARROLL	vase	A-5 Section

McCARROLL

McCLAY	2 vases in white chain railings	A-2 Section

1st Vase
McCLAY
2nd Vase
in loving memory of William 18 January 1963
also his wife Mary Elizabeth 30 July 1971
McCLAY
Wm Francis died 7 August 1991

McCLAY	see McNeilly	A-5 Section

McCLAY	black stone and surround	A-6 Section

McCLAY

McCLAY	heavy low stone	No 096 OLD Section

McCLAY
on map - Jas McNeice, Francis McClay and James McClay

McCLAY	tall stone and railings	No 155 OLD Section

erected by Joseph McClay in memory of his beloved wife
Jane died 20 January 1878 aged 63 years also his son
Robert James died 5 January 1858 aged 3 months also the above
Joseph McClay died 25 December 1891 aged 81 years also
Elizabeth the beloved wife of John McClay died 18 October 1894 aged 41
years also their son
John, husband of Gearginna (sic) McClay died 27 May 1928
on map - J McElroy

McCLEAN	black headstone	A-3 Section

McCLEAN
in loving memory of a devoted wife and mother
Elizabeth Jane died 21 October 1970

McCLEAN	stone and surround	A-5 Section

McCLEAN
in loving memory of our dear mother
Elizabeth died 3 October 1976
her mother Ellen McKaig died 11 December 1945
and sister Martha McKaig died 22 November 1955
The Lord is my shepherd

| McCLEAN | granite cross on pedestal | A-8 Section |

McCLEAN
in loving memory of our dear parents
David Green died 2 March 1952
Rachel Jane died 12 April 1952
Remembered always

| McCLEAN | see Bailie | A-11 Section |

| McCLEERY | see Bigger | A-13 Section |

| McCLELLAND | see Parker | No 162 OLD Section |

| McCLOY | grey granite | A-2 Section |

McCLOY
precious memories of our dear parents
Rebecca nee Montgomery died 6 January 1954 aged 74
Andrew died 7 April 1963 aged 82 also their daughter-in-law
Agnes nee McGladdery died 3 May 1987 aged 78
beloved wife of David

| McCLOY | white stone in railings | A-5 Section |

McCLOY
in loving memory of my dear wife
Sarah Jane died 15 July 1958 also her husband and our dear father
Spence McCloy died 21 May 1959
Thy will be done

| McCOMB | see McCrum | A-8 Section |

| McCONNELL | see McCrum | A-8 Section |

| McCORMICK | grey urn | A-8 Section |

McCORMICK

| McCORMICK | black marble in surround | No 063A OLD Section |

here lieth the body of John McCormick of Carnmoney
who departed this life 16 August 1815 aged 68 years also his wife
Mary McCormick who departed this life 28 April 1808 aged 56 years also
Lydia McCormick dearly beloved wife of John McCormick
died 7 July 1912 aged 52 years
on map - McCormick

| McCORMICK | black granite and surround | No 063B OLD Section |

the family burying ground of the late John McCormick
Carnmoney

| McCORMICK | small white vase | No 063C OLD Section |

Samuel McCormick died 20 December 1975

| McCREA | white marble and iron surround | A-2 Section |

erected in memory of my dear husband
Samuel McCrea who died 29 November 1935
also my grand-daughter Sybil who died 15 January 1936
also his wife Mary Jane McCrea who died 18 November 1939
also Sarah Morrison died 9 May 1957
also Henry Barnett who died 8 October 1974 aged 82 also his
beloved wife Mary Margaret Barnett who died 27 October 1981 aged 85 years

---

| McCREA | grey stone and surround | A-3 Section |

McCREA
Robert a loved husband and father died 14 August 1990

| McCREA | headstone and railings | A-12 Section |

in loving memory of our dear mother
Margaret McCrea who died 18 February 1936 also our dear father
Thomas James McCrea who died 10 September 1946

| MCCRUM | double marble & surround | A-1 Section |

McCrum
in loving memory of Samuel McCrum, Kilcreel
died 11th February 1897 aged 55 years interred in Carnmoney
also his wife Elizabeth died 25th December 1927 aged 82 years
"Thy will be done"
Left surround
also their son James died 27th September 1957
beloved husband of Margaret McCrum
also their daughter Elizabeth McCrum died 13th November 1964
Right surround
also their son Samuel died 2nd October 1915 aged 37 years
interred in Kinistino, Canada
also their daughter Mary who died 31st October 1945
Bottom surround
also their daughter Agnes died 23 September 1971 also
Margaret wife of James McCrum died 23 February 1976
At rest

| McCRUM | see Porter | A-2 Section |

| McCRUM | black stone | A-2 Section |

McCRUM
Kilgreel
in loving memory of Elizabeth died 9 May 1987

| McCRUM | grey granite stone | A-3 Section |

McCRUM
in loving memory of Samuel died 16 March 1957
beloved husband of Elizabeth McCrum, Millbank also the above
Elizabeth died 4 April 1967 also
William Scott died 27 February 1983
The Lord is my shepherd

| McCRUM | grey marble stone and surround | A-8 Section |

McCRUM
erected by William B McCrum, Kilcreel, Templepatrick
in loving memory of his wife
Agnes McConnell who died 13 September 1920 also his wife
Jane McComb who died 18 May 1940 also the above
William B McCrum who died 2 January 1957
Side - also their son James who died 30 September 1912

| McCRUM | marble stone and surround | A-12 Section |

McCRUM
in loving memory of our dear mother
Agnes McCrum who died 2 December 1947 also our dear father
Joseph McCrum who died 20 March 1951 also their son
James who died 25 September 1991

| McCULLOUGH | see Junk | A-13 Section |

| McCUTCHEON | granite stone, vase and surround | A-5 Section |

McCUTCHEON
in loving memory of William James
beloved husband of Maria McCutcheon died 28 September 1944
also our dear daughter Maria Elizabeth died in infancy also his wife
Maria died 21 March 1966
Loving thoughts

| McDONALD | vase and grey surround | A-9 Section |

McDONALD

| McDOWELL | headstone | A-6 Section |

McDOWELL
in loving memory of my dear husband
Samuel who died 9 May 1976

| McDOWELL | vase | A-8 Section |

Ellen McDowell from Rose

| McDOWELL | see Woods | A-8 Section |

| McELROY | see McClay | No 155 OLD Section |

| McGAW | carved stone in railings | No 042A OLD Section |

sacred to the memory of
John Thoburn McGaw who died April 15 1836 aged 41 years also his son
Robert Campbell McGaw who died May 12 1835 aged 8 years
Margaret Guthrie wife to the above named John T McGaw
died July 11 1879 aged 87 years
William John McGaw died in Australia July 11 1894 aged 59 years
Joseph McGaw died in England May 14 1898 aged 69 years
on map - Rev McGaw

| McGAW | upright stone in railings | No 042B OLD Section |

erected by Joseph McGaw in memory of his son
Robert who died 28 May 1805 aged 15 years and his daughter
Elizabeth who died 18 May 1818 aged 18 years
the said Joseph McGaw died 2 May 1836 aged 76 years
Letitia Thoburn his wife died 1 October 1838 aged 78 years
on map - Mary McGaw

| McGAW | carved stone in railings | No 042C OLD Section |

in memory of William Orr McGaw of Sunnyside
who died 16 June 1885 aged 87 years
Agnes his wife (daughter of the Rev Alexander Clarke, Lylehill)
who died 1 May 1843 aged 32 years
Alexander Clarke their son who died 13 June 1848 aged 10 years
Mary their daughter who died 19 January 1925 aged 89 years

| McGLADDERY | stone open book | A-2 Section |

in loving memory of my sister Cassie
Vase
McGLADDERY

| McGLADDERY | black marble stone | A-2 Section |

in loving memory of a devoted husband and father
William who died 4 July 1982

| McGLADDERY | see McCloy | A-2 Section |

McGLADDERY	black marble vase	A-2 Section
	McGLADDERY	

McGLADDERY	no stone	No 120 OLD Section
	on map - John McGladdery	

McGLADDERY	no stone	No 141 OLD Section
	on map - John McGladdery	

McGLADE	see Platt	A-11 Section

McGRATH	see Cornett	A-3 Section

McGREADY	large fallen stone under tree	No 074 OLD Section

erected by James McGready in memory of
Maggie Jannet and James who were interred in Mearns...... yard
Samuel, Mary, Jane and Susan who died in infancy
? R Mary aged 11 years and Maggie 17 years beloved by all
Fell asleep in Jesus
"? shall feed his flock like a ?
? he shall gather the lambs
arm and carry them in his arms "
his eldest daughter Agnes wife of James Caruth died 5 March 1886
Three of his grandchildren who died in infancy
his beloved wife Margaret died 4 September 1888
also the above James McGready died 24 August 1896
and on a small urn
McGready
father
27 July 1919
mother
10 February 1950
At rest
on map - Jas McGrady

McGRUGAN	grey marble stone and surround	A-6 Section

McGRUGAN
in loving memory of my dear husband
Andrew Nesbitt died 23 February 1978 also his wife
Mary Elizabeth (Cis) died 17 August 1994
Redeemed
Vase McGRUGAN

McILRAITH	metal plaque	No 149B OLD Section
	erected by their daughters	

McILRAITH	stone and railings	No 149C OLD Section

erected by Sarah McIlraith of Greencastle in memory of her beloved husband
John McIlraith who departed this life 18 November 1874 aged 74 years
also their son Thomas who died 18 September 1857 aged 2 years also their
daughter Sarah McIlraith who departed this life 20 August 1892 aged 42 yrs
also the above named Sarah McIlraith
who departed this life 5 November 1904 aged 84 years

McILROY	black marble urn	A-2 Section
	McILROY	

McILWAINE	no stone	No 017 OLD Section
	on map - S McIlwaine	

McILWAINE	no stone	No 079 OLD Section
	on map - Anna and Sarah McIlwaine	

| McILWRATH | metal shield and railings | No 149A OLD Section |

the family burying ground of
Hugh McIlwrath, Ballysillan
on map - J McIlwrath

| McINTYRE | grey granite stone | A-3 Section |

McINTYRE
in loving memory of our dear daughter
Roberta died 20 March 1962 and her loving mother
Lilian died 8 July 1974 and her dear father
Thomas died 3 March 1980
The Lord is my shepherd
Glass covered flowers mention
Brother Billy, Uncle John and Aunt Meta, Lilian and Geoff,
Uncle Jack and Aunt Reta and Auntie Annie

| McKAIG | see McClean | A-5 Section |

| McKEEN | small black stone | A-8 Section |

McKEEN
in loving memory of David died 9 February 1939
and his wife Agnes died 28 April 1942

| McKEEN | large fallen stone | No 037 OLD Section |

too heavy to be lifted
on map - Thomas McKeen

| McKEOWN | white marble in railings | A-1 Section |

McKeown
in memory of my beloved brother
Willie Foster died 24th August 1929
also my beloved daughter Meta Park died 26th October 1938
also my dear husband John McKeown died 17th May 1957
and his dear wife Rachael died 22nd August 1972
and Black Vase
"McKeown"

| McKEOWN | badly worn slate stone | No 096A OLD Section |

wording all flaked away
on map - Mrs McKeown

| McKNIGHT | see Crothers | A-4 Section |

| McKNIGHT | see Barbour | A-7 Section |

| McLARNON | marble headstone | A-6 Section |

McLARNON
in loving memory of a dear husband and father
Henry died 10 June 1979 also a dear wife and mother
Letitia May died 15 September 1993
Lovingly remembered

| McLAUGHLIN | no stone | No 152 OLD Section |

on map - Ann, John and James McLaughlin

| McMEEKIN | double black stones and surround | A-8 Section |

in loving memory of Hugh Semple McMeekin died 21 April 1941
his wife Margaret McCord McMeekin died 4 October 1948
their daughter Sophia Owens McMeekin died 17 October 1919
their son Hugh Semple McMeekin died 14 March 1977
their daughter Andrey Moyra Irwin died 23 December 1978

| McMICHAEL | grey stone in railings | A-11 Section |

McMICHAEL
in loving memory of our dear daughter
Martha who died 26 August 1901 also our dear son
James who died 2 April 1923 also my dear wife
Mary McMichael who died 28 January 1951

| McMILLAN | black marble | A-1 Section |

McMillan
in loving memory of our dear father
William who died 5th February 1927
his son-in-law James Fairfield who died 14th May 1993

| McMILLAN | grey marble vase | A-2 Section |

McMILLAN

| McMILLAN | stone | A-5 Section |

McMILLAN
in loving memory of my dear husband
William died 29 September 1971 also his father
Robert died 1959 and his mother
Joanna died 1961 also
Letitia Jane dear wife of the above William
died 30 October 1991

| McMILLAN | stone and surround | A-5 Section |

in loving memory of
Andrew M McMillan, Ballyvesey, died 29 August 1938 aged 83 years
also his wife Annie Crozier died 19 April 1945 aged 90 years
also their son George McMillan died 25 October 1961 aged 74 years
their daughter Elizabeth Johnstone McMillan died 13 March 1968 aged 84 years
their daughter-in-law Letitia McMillan died 4 May 1970 aged 79 years
their daughter Eleanor McMillan died 29 June 1980 aged 91 years

---

| McMILLAN | grey stone | A-6 Section |

McMILLAN
in loving memory of my dear wife and our devoted mother
Margaret Jane died 10 April 1974 also her dear husband
Samuel died 17 June 1983
At rest

| McMILLAN | grey granite stone | A-6 Section |

McMILLAN
in loving memory of a dear husband and father
Robert died 23 August 1988
My Redeemer liveth

| McMILLEN | headstone and surround | A-8 Section |

erected in loving memory of
William McMillen died 5 May 1921 also his wife
Martha Elizabeth died 16 August 1946, their daughter
Sarah Elizabeth Nicholl died 16 December 1963
Thy will be done

| McMILLEN | white marble stone in railings | A-8 Section |

erected by James McMillen of Springhill, Nova Scotia
in loving memory of his mother
Ellen McMillen who departed this life 28 March 1911 also his brother
Robert H. McMillen who departed this life 5 October 1910 also his brother
Samuel McMillen who departed this life 22 January 1919 also his father
Henry McMillen who departed this life 22 January 1926 also his sister
Elizabeth Jane McMillen who departed this life 13 October 1933 also his
sister Rebecca McMillen who departed this life 14 December 1963 also his
niece Margaret Hull died 22 March 1979
Thy will be done

| MILLAR | granite stone and surround | A-9 Section |

MILLAR
in loving memory of my dear parents
Mary died 15 May 1934
John died 29 December 1967

| MILLAR | grey marble stone | A-9 Section |

MILLAR
in loving memory of my dear husband
Thomas died 5 June 1978
The Lord is my shepherd

| MILLAR | grey granite stone and surround | A-11 Section |

erected in memory of
Myrtie (sic) the dearly loved daughter of Robert R. and Mary Millar
who fell asleep in Jesus on 19 June 1921 aged 23 years
She always made home happy
and their sons
Robert R. who passed away on 19 October 1888 aged 2
David J. who passed away 4 May 1898 aged 3 also tha above named
Robert R. Millar died 29 August 1922 aged 68 years and
Mary his wife died 2 September 1929 aged 76 also their son
Joseph Millar died 25 February 1947 aged 66 also their son-in-law
William John Gillespie died 11 January 1957 aged 74

| MILLER | worn grey stone in railings | A-2 Section |

MILLER
in loving memory of our dear father
Robert Miller died 27 May 1935 also our dear mother
Ann Jane Miller died 24 October 1943

| MILLIGAN | red granite stone and surround | A-11 Section |

the family burying ground of James Milligan

| MILTON | white cross and surround | A-12 Section |

in loving memory of
Christabel Florence Rice daughter of E.J. & M.A.Milton
who died 16 March 1903 aged 18 years
Blessed are the pure in heart for they shall see God

| MITCHELL | 3 black urns | A-3 Section |

MITCHELL George 20 April 1975
CUMMINGS Sarah   4 April 1980
ANDERSON

| MOAT | see Herivel | A-3 Section |

| MOAT | grey marble & iron surround | No 027 OLD Section |

Erected by James and John Moat of Belfast in memory of
Joseph A Moat died 8 November 1824 aged 24 years
James Moat Junr. died 5 January 1826 aged 28 years
Mary Moat Hope died 6 February 1826 aged 32 years
Samuel Moat Sen. died 9 February 1827 aged 34 years
Jane Moat died 25 January 1831 aged 68 years
James Moat Senr. died 19 February 1838 aged 85 years
John Moat Senr. died 17 August 1854 aged 56 years
Samuel Moat Junr. died 26 July 1863 aged 17 years
Anne Moat died 28 February 1886 aged 78 years
Samuel James Moat died at California 12 January 1890 aged 7 1/2 years
Joseph A Moat died 6 September 1891 aged 58 years
James Moat died 21 October 1896 aged 61 years
John Moat died 5 April 1916 aged 67 years
Annie E Moat died 18 February 1922 aged 43 years
Sarah Moat died 14 May 1958 aged 101 years
Martha C Moat died 7 February 1963 aged 82 years
metal shield
the family burying ground of James Moat
on map - James and John Moat

MOFFATT	see Chambers	A-11 Section

MOGEY	black marble stone	A-5 Section

MOGEY
in loving memory of our dear father
Richard died 14 October 1942 also our dear mother
Mary died 11 November 1975
The Lord is my shepherd
Black vase - MOGEY

MOGEY	black stone	A-6 Section

MOGEY
in loving memory of Eileen died 1 November 1992
Mark Richard died 22 January 1964
Catherine E. (Elsie) died 24 November 1945
There is a Redeemer

MOGEY	grey marble stone	A-8 Section

in loving memory of
William H Mogey who died 30 January 1922 and his wife
Agnes who died 19 October 1929 also their daughter
Martha Marcus Crowe who died 26 March 1967 and their son
Thomas John who died 15 January 1972 also his loving wife
Elizabeth who died 22 January 1976
Vase   MOGEY

MOGEY	black stone	A-14 Section

MOGEY
in loving memory of a devoted husband, father and grandfather
William Marshall who died 8 June 1985
The day Thou gavest, Lord, is ended

MONTGOMERY	white marble stone	A-2 Section

MONTGOMERY
in loving memory of our dear parents
Thomas Carroll Montgomery died 16 January 1933
Martha Rodwell Montgomery died 18 May 1976 also their daughter-in-law
Hannah Mary died 7 September 1994
At rest

MONTGOMERY	see McCloy	A-2 Section

MONTGOMERY	square black vase	A-3 Section

Billy Montgomery 8 December 1980

MONTGOMERY	black marble surround	A-5 Section

the family burying ground of
James Montgomery

MONTGOMERY	limestone and railings	A-5 Section

in loving memory of Andrew
beloved husband of Annie Montgomery
killed by enemy action 16 April 1941
also his dear wife Annie who died 17 November 1952

MONTGOMERY	grey marble stone	A-5 Section

MONTGOMERY
in loving memory of my dear husband
Alexander called home 10 November 1957
ever remembered by his loving wife and daughter Anna
also his dear wife Anna died 5 June 1975
In heavenly live abiding

MONTGOMERY	grey marble stone and surround	A-6 Section

MONTGOMERY

MONTGOMERY	black marble surround	A-7 Section

MONTGOMERY
Black vase   MONTGOMERY

MONTGOMERY	white broken stone in railings	A-10 Section

MONTGOMERY
in loving memory of Elizabeth died 30 January 1946 and her husband
Joseph killed in action 27 August 1916 interred in Belgium
also their son Andrew died 22 July 1968
At rest

MONTGOMERY	square vase	A-10 Section

MONTGOMERY

MONTGOMERY	Limestone with iron surround	No 148 OLD Section

erected by Joseph Montgomery, Ballyveasey in memory of his father
Isaac Montgomery who departed this life 23 October 1869 aged 82 years
also his mother
Elizabeth Montgomery who departed this life 28 December 1858 aged 66 years
also his brother
Isaac Montgomery who departed this life 26 February 1836 aged 6 years
"O may our feet pursue the way
Our pious parents led
With love and holy zeal obey
The counsels of the dead.
Far from this world of toil and strife
They're present with the Lord
The labours of their mortal life
End in a large reward."
on map - Jas and Joseph Montgomery

MONTGOMERY	Limestone stone with plinth	No 169 OLD Section

erected by Joseph Montgomery in memory of his children
Elizabeth Elleanor who died 23 January 1889 aged 7 years
Andrew who died 28 November 1889 aged 6 years
Elleanor Georgina died 31 July 1896 aged 3 years
James died 22 May 1897 aged 2 years
William died 9 June 1899 aged 21 years
Josephine died 29 October 1905 aged 3 months
Mary died 12 August 1910 aged 22 years
also above
Joseph Montgomery who died 8 July 1922 aged 67 years
also his wife
Elizabeth who died 1 October 1926 aged 70 years
on map - Jas Montgomery

MONTGOMERY	grey stone with railings	No 174 OLD Section

erected by William John Montgomery in loving memory of his wife
Martha died 2 December 1934 also the above
William John Montgomery died 14 June 1936
on map - Wm Montgomery

MOORE	black marble	A-1 Section

MOORE
cherished memories of Robert (Bob)
a devoted husband father and grandfather
died 1st September 1994
Abide with me

MOORE	triple plot with surround	A-4 Section

MOORE

MOORE	see Brown	A-5 Section

MOORE	black vase	A-6 Section

Mary Ann Moore 27 December 1984
and Jim Moore 20 January 1971
Redeemed

MOORE	see Ferguson	No 145 OLD Section

MORELAND	see Hamill	A-8 Section

MORRISON	see McCrea	A-2 Section

MORRISON	triple marble edged plot	A-7 Section

in memory of my husband Samuel Morrison died February 1919
also my daughter Agnes Morrison died 11 June 1914
and son Samuel died 13 October 1920
Georgina Morrison died 17 April 1941
Annie Morrison died 7 January 1942
Arthur Morrison died 28 June 1967

MORROW	black urn	A-9 Section

MORROW

MORTON	grey marble & surround	A-1 Section

in loving memory of
Caroline beloved wife of George Morton
who entered into rest 6th February 1929

MORTON	white marble stone in railings	A-9 Section

in loving memory of
Thomas dearly loved husband of M.J.Morton died 7 June 1939
Victor C.Morton devoted husband and father called home 5 November 1962
also his beloved wife Mabel died 9 August 1981
With Christ which is far better

MULHOLLAND	no stone	No 131 OLD Section

on map - Wm John Mulholland

MULHOLLAND	large low granite, urn and crosses	No 151 OLD Section

MULHOLLAND
in loving memory of my dear husband Thomas who died 20 January 1947
also my dear son James who died 21 May 1937
also Annie H wife of above Thomas died 25 April 1964
Urn   Mulholland
white cross 11 July W Mulholland 1961 R.E.M
white cross 19 July M Mulholland 1968 R.E.M
on map - Thos Mulholland

MULHOLLAND	no stone	No 156 OLD Section

on map - J Mulholland

MULHOLLAND	no stone	No 156A OLD Section

on map - T Mulholland

MULHOLLAND	no stone	No 156B OLD Section

on map - J Mulholland

MULLAN	see Hope	No 050 OLD Section

| MULVENNA | see Gourley | A-6 Section |

| MURDOCH | grey stone | No 110A OLD Section |

this stone and burial place belongeth to
James Murdoch of Belfast
here lyeth the body of his wife Elizabeth Murdoch
who departed this life 25 October 1770 aged 26 years
also two of their children Robert and James

| MURDOCH | fallen stone in surround | No 119 OLD Section |

on stone - Alex Murdock - but too heavy to lift to read remainder
on map - Alex Murdoch

| MURDOCK | see Kell | A-11 Section |

| MURPHY | grey granite surround in large plot | A-9 Section |

MURPHY

| MURRAY | metal shield | No 040 OLD Section |

the burial place of James Murray
1894
on map - Janet Murray

| NAWN | grey marble stone and surround | A-6 Section |

NAWN
in loving memory of our dear parents
Charles Fleming died 4 October 1952
Catherine died 19 April 1975
Vase NAWN

| NELSON | headstone | A-8 Section |

NELSON
in loving memory of a beloved wife and mother Elizabeth (Lizzie)
died 27 August 1914 aged 27 also her infant sons and her darling daughter
Margaret (Babs) died 11 January 1924 aged 18
Erected by Norah Gilmore
In God's keeping

| NELSON | triple surround | A-11 Section |

NELSON

| NESBITT | stone and railings | No 142 OLD Section |

in loving memory of William Nesbitt died 10 October 1891 also his son
John Nesbitt died 31 March 1913 and his son's wife
Jane Eliza Nesbitt died 3 November 1914
on map - John E Nesbitt
Anne and Vance Parkers

| NESBITT | large stone in railings | No 143A OLD Section |

erected by David Nesbitt, Mallusk in memory of his son
David who died August 1 1827 aged 19 years also his son
John who died April 10 1845 aged 41 years also two infant children
James Hope Nesbitt died 4 September 1927 aged 74 years
NESBITT

NESBITT	large obelisk, stone and railings	No 143B OLD Section

erected by Thomas Nesbitt of Belfast in memory of his beloved wife
Anna Matilda Sherlock who died 5 June 1893 aged 67 years
the above named Thomas H Nesbitt who died 17 March 1901 in his 77th year
his mother-in-law Martha Courtney who died 20 September 1878 aged 86 yrs
his father-in-law William Courtney who died 10 November 1879 aged 82 yrs
his son-in-law William J Bradwen Jones who died 23 July 1910 aged 57 yrs
his grandson Thomas Nesbitt Bradwen Jones who died 20 July 1933 aged 33 yrs
Who shall separate us from the love of Christ. Rom VIII, 35
NESBITT
on map - Thos Nesbitt

NESBITT	tall grey stone	No 144 OLD Section

erected by Samuel Nesbitt, Mallusk in memory of his son
David who died September 30 1845 aged 11 months
in memory of Margaret Nesbitt beloved wife of Alex Officer Nesbitt
who died 24 November 1905 aged 53 years also the above
Alex Officer Nesbitt who died 17 January 1931 aged 79 years
on map - Alex Nesbitt

NICHOLL	see McMillen	A-8 Section

NICHOLL	granite stone and surround	A-11 Section

NICHOLL
in loving memory of our dear parents
Louisa Nicholl who died 24 October 1946
William Nicholl who died 15 April 1958, their dear son
Herbert James Nicholl who died 18 October 1968 beloved husband of
Edith who died 5 April 1982, their dear daughter
Annie who died 2 June 1969

NIMMONS	triple railed enclosure	A-7 Section

erected by John Nimmons in loving memory of his father
Alexander Nimmons died 3 November 1926 also his wife
Susan Gray died 9 January 1920 and his daughter
Martha Nimmons died 8 April 1919
Large wooden cross   Annie Hunter
another stone   no name

O'NEILL	black vase	A-8 Section

O'NEILL
Jessie 14.6.90
William 8.8.73

O'NEILL	white stone and surround	A-11 Section

in loving memory of
Sarah O'Neill who died 27 April 1913 also her son
Hugh O'Neill who died 10 January 1904, her daughter
Kathleen O'Neill who died 1 June 1916
R.I.P.

OFFICER	white marble stone and surround	A-2 Section

OFFICER
in loving memory of our dear parents
Eleanor Jane died 10 January 1951
Thomas May died 29 May 1951 also their loving daughter
Doris Logan died 15 July 1991
Till we meet

OFFICER	no stone	No 014 OLD Section

on map - David and Sarah Officer

ORCHIN	no stone	No 035 OLD Section

on map - Eleanor Orchin

ORR	see Rankin	A-8 Section

PARK	see McKeown	A-1 Section

PARKER	white marble	A-2 Section

PARKER
in loving memory of Ellen beloved wife of Thomas Parker
fell asleep 18 February 1944 also son
Wesley fell asleep 8 September 1945 also the above
Thomas Parker fell asleep 3 December 1951 also their daughter-in-law
Jeannie Parker called home 16 December 1984
At rest

PARKER	small flat painted rock	A-3 Section

Nelson Parker

PARKER	headstone and surround	A-11 Section

in loving memory of
Agnes beloved wife of Thomas Parker died 15 July 1935 also her dear
husband Thomas died 27 September 1967

PARKER	tall limestone	No 069A OLD Section

erected to the memory of John Parker of Sheepheads
who died in the Lord on the 3 February 1856 aged 73 years also his son
Thomas who died in the sure and certain hope of a glorious resurrection
unto eternal life on the 19 August 1840 aged 28 years also his daughter
Sarah who died in the Lord on the 23 January 1849 aged 18 years also
his daughter Janet who died young in December 1836 also his beloved wife
Margaret who died in the Lord on the 12 September 1867 aged 77 years also
his son Matthew died 11 October 1878 aged 56 years
on map - Thos Parker

PARKER	tall limestone	No 069B OLD Section

erected to the memory of Benjamin B Parker of Sheep Heads
who departed this life 11 April 1874 aged 36 years also his brother
John died 14 October 1880 aged 66 years also his brother
David who died 27 January 1892 aged 71 years

PARKER	fallen stone - white marble	No 070 OLD Section

erected by Joseph Parker of Sheepheads in loving memory of his son
John who died 21 May 1896 aged 19 years also his wife
Margaret who departed this life 7 March 1903 aged 63 years also the above
Joseph Parker who died 14 February 1910 aged 85 years also their daughter
Margaret wife of Thomas Gordon who died 12 February 1950
on map - Thos. Robinson

PARKER	granite headstone	No 094 OLD Section

here lyeth the body of Robert Parker of Bellnabernise
who departed this life 17 February 1799 aged 94 years also
Jannet Parker allies M ..... ell his spouse who departed this life
26 April 1791 .... 77 ? years ... he son
John Parker who departed this life 1 May 1782 aged 42 years

PARKER	metal shield and railings	No 101 OLD Section

the family burying ground of Wm Parker

PARKER   granite stone and surround   No 162 OLD Section

PARKER
in loving memory of
William Henry Parker, Ballyutoag, who died 19 February 1942
his wife Agnes died 21 May 1961 and their sons
F/O John Parker R.A.F.V.R
missing presumed dead air operations over Germany 23 July 1944
Robert Carson Parker died 12 December 1987
Left side
Jane McClelland wife of Parker Carson died 11 July 1897 interred in Rashee
Parker Carson died 12 April 1844
Right side
Robert Carson died 29 June 1902
on map - Wm Carson

PARKERS   see Nesbitt   No 142 OLD Section

PARKHILL   vary tall black marble stone   No 108B OLD Section

PARKHILL
this stone was erected by bequest of William Parkhill
who died 14 May 1904 aged 55 years
here were also interred his mother and father
Jane Parkhill who died 25 May 1887 aged 72
Robert Parkhill who died 1 December 1887 aged 86
also his sister
Jane Parkhill who died in the year 1858 aged 8 also
Elizabeth Fee wife of Joseph Parkhill who died 7 April 1883 aged 25 years
also his brothers
James Parkhill who died 28 March 1865 aged 22 years
David Parkhill who died 21 January 1868 aged 23 years
Robert Parkhill who died in the year 1888 aged 35 years
Joseph Parkhill who died 12 November 1892 aged 38 years
on map - Jas Porkhill

PARKILL   square limestone   No 108A OLD Section

in memory of his brother James Parkill
who departed this life 30 March 1847 aged 48 years

PARKILL   limestone - ornate top   No 108C OLD Section

erected by James Parkill in memory of his wife
Janet who departed this life on 15 October 1833 aged 62 years

---

PARKS   double black stones and surround   A-3 Section

PARKS
in loving memory of our dear parents
Francis who died 23 October 1963
Margaret who died 5 April 1986 also our dear aunt
Janet Bigger who died 18 August 1965
At rest with God

PATTERSON   white marble stone   A-2 Section

PATTERSON
in loving memory of our dear father
William who died 11 November 1948 also our dear mother
Sadie who died 14 September 1965
Jesus understands

PATTERSON   small white square vase   A-4 Section

John C L Patterson 2.8.89

PATTERSON   black marble stone   A-6 Section

PATTERSON
in loving memory of
our dear mother Mary (Minnie) died 20 January 1952
our dear father Robert Edward died 6 December 1956
our dear sister Hannah Elizabeth died 27 September 1968

PATTERSON	no stone	No 105 OLD Section
	on map - Agnes Patterson	

PATTERSON	see Glass	No 106 OLD Section

PATTON	see Taylor	A-6 Section

PEDEN	no stone	No 030 OLD Section
	on map - Hugh Peden	

PLATT	granite stone and triple surround	A-11 Section

PLATT
in loving memory of
John M.Platt who died 25 January 1933, his wife
Matilda M.H.M. who died 16 March 1913, their son
Abraham who died 19 February 1900 also
Abraham Platt brother of John M. who died 18 August 1901
Sarah Jane Platt born 28 July 1883 died 17 May 1962
interred Arlington Cemetery, Drexel Hill, PA, USA
Until the day breaks
erected by family
Left edge
Emily M. wife of Samuel B. Black born 20 January 1899 died 22 February 1952
interred Arlington Cemetery, Drexel Hill, PA, USA
Florence E. wife of Joshua McGlade born 13 January 1889 died 23 Nov 1937
interred Carnmoney Cemetery
Right edge
also their son Robert John who died 19 February 1928
interred in Dundonald Cemetery
Olive N.M. wife of Arthur Brothwell born 10 June 1892 died 13 Nov 1950
Back edge
Margaret wife of John Davison born 7 August 1896 died 18 October 1958
interred Greenwood Cemetery, Alberni, Canada

PORKHILL	see Parkhill	No 108B OLD Section

PORTER	white stone and railings	A-2 Section

in loving memory of my dear husband
Samuel Porter who died 19 November 1935 also his dear wife
Elizabeth Porter who died 25 August 1941 also their daughter
Agnes McCrum died 22 January 1991 aged 82 years
At rest

PRESSDEE	round black vase	A-5 Section
	PRESSDEE	

PRESTON	square black vase	A-5 Section
	PRESTON	

PRESTON	stone cross	A-6 Section
	PRESTON	

QUERN	see Gilmore	A-1 Section

QUINN	no stone	No 033 OLD Section
	on map - Mrs Quinn	

RANKIN	black marble vase	A-8 Section
	RANKIN, BIRKMYRE, ORR	

| REA | black marble stone and vase | A-2 Section |

REA
in loving memory of Frank who died 11 May 1935
also his dear wife Sarah who died 5 March 1956
Treasured memories of Isabel who died 30 November 1984
beloved wife of Sammy
Vase   REA

| REA | grey stone and surround | A-3 Section |

REA
in loving memory of my dear husband and our devoted father
William Allen died 12 July 1978 aged 82 years

| REA | black headstone | A-3 Section |

REA
in loving memory of a dear husband and father
Henry (Harry) died 15 December 1990

| REA | black stone | A-3 Section |

REA
in loving memory of Alexander (Sandy)
a loving husband and dear father died 4 May 1990
Will always be remembered.

| REA | see Hamilton | A-6 Section |

| REA | see Johnston | No 061 OLD Section |

| REID | black vase | A-8 Section |

Robert Reid

| REID | see Finlay | No 173 OLD Section |

| RHODES | see McCammond | A-5 Section |

| ROBERTS | white marble and railings | A-6 Section |

ROBERTS
in loving memory of Edward beloved husband of Annie Roberts
who died 12 September 1949 also the above
Annie who died 24 December 1977
Till we meet

| ROBINSON | black marble stone and surround | A-3 Section |

ROBINSON
in loving memory of David born 25 October 1897 died 21 January 1984
Ann Jane born 15 August 1896 died 19 February 1985

| ROBINSON | small grey stone | A-3 Section |

ROBINSON
in loving memory of my husband
Joseph Alexander born 4 June 1920 died 23 November 1987
Worthy of everlasting remembrance

| ROBINSON | black urn | A-4 Section |

ROBINSON

| ROBINSON | white headstone | A-11 Section |

in loving memory of my parents
Samuel and Agnes Robinson and my dear sister May
also my dear wife Eleanor died 6 August 1969
a devoted wife and mother

| ROBINSON | white stone and surround | A-12 Section |

erected by Joseph Robinson in loving memory of his daughter
Ann Jane who died 25 October 1931 aged 14 years, the above
Jos. Robinson who died 27 March 1937
Gone but not forgotten
also his dear wife Elizabeth who died 30 November 1942
Forever in our thoughts
also Thos. Robinson died 1 May 1937
Peace, perfect peace

| ROBINSON | black marble stone and surround | A-13 Section |

ROBINSON
in loving memory of our beloved parents
John Archibald died 13 December 1978
Eleanor Elizabeth died 6 August 1969

| ROBINSON | black marble stone and surround | A-14 Section |

ROBINSON
in loving memory of
Parker beloved husband, father and grandfather died 30 August 1991

| ROBINSON | black marble decorated stone | No 019 OLD Section |

in loving memory of my dear husband
Hugh J Robinson who died 8 November 1918
on map - John Robinson

| ROBINSON | see Parker | No 070 OLD Section |

| ROBINSON | no stone | No 093 OLD Section |

on map - Wm Robinson

| ROSS | small white square vase | A-7 Section |

in loving memory
Edward Ross 15.2.88
Mary Ross 13.4.63

| ROSS | small stone | A-10 Section |

in loving memory of my dear mother Mary Ross
also my dear father Hugh Ross
also my dear brother John Ross
also my dear daughter Ruby Hawthorne died 2 May 1920

| ROWAN | no stone | No 031 OLD Section |

on map - T Rowan

| RUSK | small grey stone in railings | A-4 Section |

in loving memory of our dear son James Rusk
who died 14 June 1925
Not forgotten

RUSSELL	limestone headstone	No 121 OLD Section

erected by John Russell of Hightown to the memory of his daughter
Janet who departed this life 8 July 1836 aged 3 years also his daughter
Sarah who died 16 May 1846 aged 20 years also his son
Hugh Giffin who died 18 May 1846 aged 10 years also his son
Alexr. Russell who died 27 March 1851 aged 20 years also the said
John Russell who died 13 September 1852 aged 86 years and his wife
Jane Giffin who died 14 August 1871 aged 77 years also their son
William Russell who died 27 May 1872 aged 44 years
on map - Jane Russell

RUSSELL	small sandstone	No 122A OLD Section

here lyeth the body of Mary Russell
who departed this life April 5, 1774 aged 40 years
on map - Joan Russell

RUSSELL	tall ornamental stone	No 122B OLD Section

erected by John Russell of Hightown in memory of his beloved wife
Sarah Wilson who died 17 September 1872 aged 44 years, the above
John Russell died 17 December 1891 aged 69 years also his son
John died 30 October 1915 aged 65 years also his son
Robert died 10 August 1922 aged 66 years also his daughter
Sarah died 17 January 1930 aged 71 years and his daughter
Mary Ann died 24 March 1949 aged 88 years

RYAN	granite stone in railings	A-9 Section

RYAN
in loving memory of our dear son
John W.Ryan who died 7 July 1922 aged 12 years also his mother
Margaret died 28 November 1946 aged 67 years

SANDS	see Walker	No 104 OLD Section

SCOTT	small kerb stone	A-2 Section

Elizabeth died 8 February 1933
Joseph died 12 May 1962
SCOTT

SCOTT	see McCrum	A-3 Section

SCOTT	headstone	A-6 Section

SCOTT
in loving memory of my dear husband
Stewart Scott died 18 April 1918
interred in Le Trepart Cemetery, France also my dear son
Joseph Bigger died 27 February 1920 also my grandson
William Skelly died 31 March 1939 also
Sarah wife of Stewart died 16 February 1968 also son
Stewart Scott died 13 January 1977
Vase Father and Mother Scott

SCOTT	see Skelly	A-6 Section

SCOTT	iron memorial and surround	A-8 Section

the family burying ground of
James Scott 1905

SCROGGIE	no stone	No 002 OLD Section

on map - Sarah Scroggie and Agnes Ireland

| SHARKEY | black iron memorial and railings | A-8 Section |

the family burying ground of
Andrew Sharkey   1931

| SHARKEY | black marble vase | A-12 Section |

SHARKEY
died 15 March 1956

| SHARKEY | headstone and railings | A-12 Section |

in loving memory of my dear husband
Chas. Sharkey who departed this life 4 May 1935

| SHARP | see Drennan | A-11 Section |

| SHERLOCK | see Nesbitt | No 143B OLD Section |

| SHERRARD | white headstone and surround | A-6 Section |

SHERRARD
in loving memory of
Alexander Sherrard, Craigarogan died 16 March 1960
also his beloved wife Hannah died 24 January 1960

| SHERRARD | grey stone and triple surround | A-6 Section |

SHERRARD
Aughnabrack House
in loving memory of
Elizabeth beloved wife of Edward Sherrard who died 1 October 1949 also
the above Edward Sherrard who died 12 September 1958 and their son
James Browne Sherrard who died 4 March 1983

| SHERRARD | grey stone | A-7 Section |

SHERRARD
in loving memory of
Elizabeth Sherrard 10 April 1916
Margaret Jane Sherrard 24 March 1951
John H Sherrard 14 April 1957
Margaret Alexandra Sherrard died 31 August 1985
Andrew Hill Sherrard died 17 November 1985
son John Sherrard died 4 January 1986

| SHERRARD | limestone - decorated top | No 124A OLD Section |

erected by Charles Sherrard, Ballyearl in memory of his wife
Mary who died 11 September 1884 aged 44 years also 2 infants
also his daughter Lizzie died 9 May 1894 aged 20 years also his daughter
Mary died 14 August 1891 aged 21 years also the above
Charles Sherrard died 23 February 1905 also his son
Samuel Sherrard died 17 March 1914
David Fee Sherrard died 17 December 1947 aged 75 years
Sarah Sherrard died 26 March 1953
on map - Sherrard

| SHERRARD | black marble stone | No 124B OLD Section |

SHERRARD
in loving memory of
Agnes died 13 November 1927
Edward died 15 December 1950
Margaret died 2 December 1977
In heavenly love abiding.

SHERRARD	white marble stone	No 124C OLD Section

SHERRARD
in loving memory of Joseph Wilson, Thrushfield, Templepatrick
beloved husband of Jane Sherrard called home 7 December 1941
also the above named Jane Sherrard died 17 April 1971 also
Wilson Sherrard born 14 October 1910 died 18 November 1986

SHERRARD	grey stone	No 124D OLD Section

erected by Andrew Sherrard, Ballyearl, in memory of his beloved wife
Dorcas Wilson who died 23 December 1899 aged 63 years
After years of sleepless watching
Borne with Christian patience
Waiting on the call of the Master
the above named Andrew Sherrard died 2 July 1903 aged 73 years

SHERRARD	iron memorial	No 124E OLD Section

the burial place of James Sherrard
Belfast 1880

SIMPSON	white marble stone and railings	A-6 Section

SIMPSON
in loving memory of my dear husband
Robert Simpson died 17 July 1947 also his dear wife
Ellen died 18 September 1953
Peace, perfect peace
Vase
in loving memory of June died 10 August 1962 aged 2
also 2 separate small white kneeling angels

SKELLY	headstone	A-6 Section

SKELLY
in loving memory of my dear husband
William died 23 April 1942 also his dear wife
Agnes died 6 July 1950 also her sister
Margaret Winchester died 27 March 1945 also
Tom Scott son of Sarah died 6 January 1987

SKELLY	see Scott	A-6 Section

SMITH	black marble stone and surround	A-2 Section

SMITH
in loving memory of my dear parents
John died 22 December 1968
Marjory died 31 May 1966 also my dear sister
May died 22 July 1963
Peace, perfect peace

SMITH	vase	A-5 Section

Georgina Smith
23 June 1980

SMITH	no stone	No 039 OLD Section

on map - John Smith

SMITH	tall limestone with iron surround	No 098 OLD Section

erected by Andrew Smith, Mossvale in memory of his wife
Jane Smith who died 23 May 1823 aged 30 years
also 2 of their children who died young, the above named
Andrew Smith died 8 April 1847 aged 68 years also his wife
Sarah Walker Smith who died 5 January 1869 aged 66 years
on map - Samuel and Andrew Smith

SMITH   large capped limestone in railings   No 099A OLD Section

1872
the burying place of George Smith, Mossvale
in memory of his children viz
George died 18 December 1861 AE 7 months
David Fulton died 30 January 1862 4 yrs 10 months
John died 11 February 1864 AE 2 yrs 8 months
Margaret Jane died 16 February 1865 AE 7 weeks
also his beloved wife
Sarah Smith who departed this life 5 December 1870 aged 40 years
also the above named
George Smith who departed this life 15 January 1889 aged 62 years also
Andrew Smith eldest son of the above named George Smith
died 20 February 1932 aged 76 years
Blessed are the dead who died in the Lord
Urn
erected by David F Smith in memory of his father 1889

SMITH   large capped limestone in railings   No 099B OLD Section

1872
erected in memory of Alexander Smith, Ballyhone
who died 30 May 1870 aged 78 years and his daughter
Martha who died 18 August 1867 aged 29 years also his wife
Mary who departed this life 11 April 1877 aged 81 years

SMITH   large black/white stone in railings   No 099C OLD Section

1902
erected in loving memory of George Smith
born at Hightown, Carnmoney 10 October 1821
died at Cragoran, Islandmagee 11 July 1900
his wife Jessie Bertram Smith
born at Gateshead-on-Tyne 23 May 1833
died at Cragoran, Islandmagee 13 February 1915
their grandson Charles Bertram son of Charles Bertram Smith
and Lizzie J Adair Smith who died 1 December 1935 aged 26 years
their greatgrandson Thomas Charles infant son of John Adair Smith and
Anne Smith of Cragoran, Islandmagee who died 23 February 1945
their son Charles Bertram Smith who died 7 November 1957 aged 94 years also
his wife Lizzie J Adair Smith died 16 January 1975 aged 98 years
Until the day break and the shadows flee away.
on map - Charles B Smith

SMITH   see Garret   No 100A OLD Section

SMITH   no stone   No 103 OLD Section

on map - Jas Smith

SMITH   no stone   No 164 OLD Section

on map - Chas Smith

SMITH   no stone   No 165 OLD Section

on map - A Smith

SMYTH   see Ellison   A-1 Section

SMYTH   grey stone in railings   A-1 Section

erected by Martha Jane Smyth in loving memory of her husband
John Smyth who died 22nd November 1943
At rest

SMYTH   grey granite and surround   A-2 Section

SMYTH
in loving memory of Hugh beloved husband of Annie Smyth, Hightown
died 19 October 1947 also his wife Annie Smyth died 30 November 1950

SMYTH	see Fullerton	A-3 Section

SMYTH	granite stone and surround	A-9 Section

SMYTH

SMYTH	vase and grey marble surround	A-9 Section

SMYTH

SMYTH	tall stone with railings	No 097 OLD Section

erected by Foster Smyth in memory of his sister
Margaret Ann died 18 March 1866 also of his father
Andrew Smyth died 16 February 1867 and of his mother
Jane Smyth died 17 July 1873 also of his brothers
Andrew John died 25 September 1872
Charles died 29 July 1891
James died 31 October 1893
William died 11 April 1895
Jane, daughter of the above named James Smyth died 23 April 1895
the above named Foster Smyth died 5 May 1900
Lizzie Frances, daughter of the above named Charles Smyth
died 13 February 1901
Edwin Charles only son of the above named Charles Smyth
died 5 April 1903 also
Jane (Jennie) Smyth daughter of the above Charles Smyth
died 15 May 1943 aged 65 years
on map - John and Wm Smith

SMYTH	flat part buried stone	No 097A OLD Section

sacred to the memory of William Smyth late of Hightown who departed this
life 1 April 1808 aged 60 years also his wife
Elonar Smyth who departed this life 3 April 1816 aged 52 years also
four of their children

SMYTH	granite with iron surround	No 098a OLD Section

erected by Samuel Smyth in memory of
his father Andrew late of Ballyearl who died 15 May 1823 aged 84 years
also his mother who died 29 July 1800 aged 60 years

SNODDY	metal shield and railings	No 086 OLD Section

the family burying ground of
John Snoddy, Cottonmount 1866
on map - R J Snoddy

SNODDY	no stone	No 087 OLD Section

on map - R J Snoddy

SPEER	tall marble stone	No 140A OLD Section

in loving memory of Sarah Speer daughter of David Speer, Carnanee
and wife of William Wilson, Ballyearl
who died 23 May 1845 aged 29 years also said
David Speer who died 18 May 1865 aged 88 years and his wife
Margaret Kennedy who died 14 February 1863 aged 88 years

SPEER	tall grey marble stone	No 140B OLD Section

erected by David and William S Speer in memory of our father
William J Speer died 15 June 1904 aged 56 years also our mother
Eliza Jane Speer died 11 March 1912 aged 68 years also the above
David died 18 June 1947, his wife
Gladys died 7 September 1971 also their son
Hyndman (Hank) died 19 June 1985 and
William died 3 March 1960 also his wife
Margaret died 5 January 1971
on map - Wm J Speer

SPEERS	black marble stone and surround	A-3 Section

SPEERS
in loving memory of a dear husband and father
Samuel James died 14 November 1973
his dear wife Isabella died 2 January 1976

SPENCE	2 black marble stones	A-9 Section

SPENCE
2nd stone
SPENCE
in loving memory of my dear husband
William died 11 January 1996
At rest

STANFIELD	see Thompson	No 044 OLD Section

STEVENSON	black urn	A-6 Section

STEVENSON

STEVENSON	black vase	No 101A OLD Section

Stevenson, William 10.2.72

STEWART	black marble stone	A-5 Section

STEWART
in loving memory of
Martha Jane born 1875 died 1938 also her husband
James born 1875 died 1945 also their son
James born 26 December 1913 died 21 November 1985
devoted husband of Isabella
Always in our thoughts
Vase STEWART

STEWART	black marble surround	A-6 Section

STEWART

STEWART	headstone and surround	A-9 Section

STEWART
erected by Catherine Stewart
in loving memory of her dear husband
A.M.Stewart died 3 May 1931

TAYLOR	granite stone and surround	A-6 Section

TAYLOR
in loving memory of my dear son
Thomas Tinsley called home 21 February 1951
Margaret Ellen Patton died 8 March 1956
also a friend of the family
Mary McCune Graham died 1 October 1967 aged 79 years
At rest

TEMPLETON	black marble	A-2 Section

TEMPLETON
in loving memory of
John Campbell died 22 March 1972 also his loving wife
Mary Jane died 8 October 1986

TEMPLETON	black marble stone	A-13 Section

TEMPLETON
ARTHUR McGLADDERY
a dearly loved husband, dad and grandad
died 5 December 1996 aged 69 years
Matt. Chap 25. V21.

TEMPLETON	see Hope	No 050A OLD Section

TEMPLETON	grey marble stone and surround	No 092A OLD Section

TEMPLETON
in loving memory of our devoted parents
Isobel died 9 September 1989
Robert died 15 March 1990
At rest.

TEMPLETON	granite stone with curved top	No 092B OLD Section

here lyeth the body of Maiy (sic) Templeton
who departed this life November 9 1776 aged 51 years
on map - John C Templeton

TEMPLETON	limestone headstone	No 129 OLD Section

erected by Joseph Templeton, Mallusk
in memory of his son
William who departed this life 23 June 1836 aged 12 years
on map - William Templeton

TEMPLETON	no stone	No 132 OLD Section

on map - Robert Templeton

THOBURN	see McGaw	No 042B OLD Section

THOBURN	see Alexander	No 059 OLD Section

THOMPSON	small square granite vase	A-3 Section

Samuel Thompson died 5 May 1973
Mary Thompson died 5 January 1986

THOMPSON	headstone, 4 stone pieces & 2 vases	A-5 Section

THOMPSON
in loving memory of
Sarah Jane Thompson died 14 October 1933 and of her husband
Robert Thompson died 23 January 1937 and their son
John Archibald Thompson died 2 August 1964 and his wife
Maria died 15 January 1984
Separate stone
in loving memory of a dear husband and father
Thomas Alexander Thompson F.R.C.O.G.
died 12 February 1991 aged 67 years
I shall arise and go to Innisfree
Separate stone
in loving memory of a dear daughter and sister
Jane Helen Marie Thompson B.Ed. died 30 April 1991 aged 35 years
Bless this little lamb tonight
Separate stone
These stones are from the family home
Downpatrick

THOMPSON	small flat stone	A-5 Section

THOMPSON
Robert 12 April 1969
Emma 11 May 1986

THOMPSON	twin white marble stones & surround	A-8 Section

THOMPSON
in loving memory

| THOMPSON | vase | A-8 Section |

Trevor Thompson
21 October 1992

| THOMPSON | black marble stone | A-9 Section |

THOMPSON
in loving memory of a devoted husband and father
Samuel died 23 January 1974

| THOMPSON | granite stone and surround | A-11 Section |

THOMPSON
in loving memory of a dear husband and devoted father
Hal died 24 December 1971 also his father
John died 8 July 1963

| THOMPSON | black stone | A-13 Section |

THOMPSON
in loving memory of our beloved mother
Irene died 14 June 1979 also her loving son
Denis died 20 July 1981

| THOMPSON | grey granite | A-13 Section |

THOMPSON
in remembrance of a dear husband and father
James who died 13 October 1908
At rest

| THOMPSON | dark grey stone | A-14 Section |

THOMPSON
in loving memory of a loving husband and devoted father
Samuel Ronald died 16 May 1993

| THOMPSON | marble headstone | No 044 OLD Section |

erected by Mary Thompson in memory of her husband
John Thompson born 3 April 1833 died 4 August 1888
her daughter Jane born 15 April 1871 died 30 August 1889
her son James born 26 October 1861 died 20 January 1906
her son Alfred born 4 October 1884 died 10 February 1909
her son Edmund born 27 February 1882 died 3 April 1919
also the above named Mary Thompson died 21 June 1924 aged 84 years
her son Samuel beloved husband of Charlotte Stanfield
died 12 February 1936 aged 60 years
and the above Charlotte S Thompson died 12 June 1967
Margaret Thompson died 26 March 1971 aged 97 years
"Till we meet"
Mary Kempston died 4 March 1945 also her husband
David K Kempston died 14 November 1949
on map - David Thorburn

| THOMPSON | no stone | No 053A OLD Section |

on map - Miss W H Thompson

| THOMPSON | no stone | No 053B OLD Section |

on map - Walter Thompson

| THOMPSON | granite stone and surround | No 054A OLD Section |

THOMPSON
erected by Percival and Martha Thompson in loving memory of their dear son
John Percival called to higher service 21 November 1949 aged 22 years
also the above Percival Thompson passed on 31 December 1961 aged 63 years
and his wife Martha died 8 April 1987 aged 87 years
on map - Martha Thompson

THOMPSON	white marble stone	No 054B OLD Section

THOMPSON
in loving memory of my dear husband
Ernest died 11 November 1973 also his devoted wife
May died 23 February 1985
on map - Ernest Thompson

THOMPSON	fallen stone	No 054C OLD Section

erected in memory of Andrew Thompson of Mulusk (sic)
who died 9 March 1820 aged 59 years also his wife
Mary who died 5 February 1837 aged 74 years also his son
Andrew who died 6 September 1837 aged 43 years
on map - 54 Lansdowne Road, Belfast

THORBURN	see Thompson	No 044 OLD Section

TIERNEY	large marble decorated in railings	No 168A OLD Section

erected by James and Eliza Tierney in memory of their dearly beloved son
Alexander who died 5 December 1885 aged 20 years also
William John who died 31 January 1871 aged 1 yr 8 months and
James who died in infancy also
Eliza beloved wife of the above James Tierney
who died 19 January 1890 aged 59 years
on map - Jas Turner

TIRNEY	metal shield	No 168B OLD Section

the family burying ground of James Tirney, Belfast 1870

TODD	see Hanna	A-3 Section

TOLLAND	granite tall stone	No 117 OLD Section

erected by Mary Tolland
in loving memory of her beloved husband
Hugh Tolland died 12 April 1910 aged 65 years
their son Andrew died 24 August 1876 aged 9 months
their daughter Isabella died 6 September 1890 aged 7 years
and of the above Mary Tolland died 20 March 1931 aged 80 years
Until the day break
TOLLAND

TOWNSLEY	black granite stone	A-7 Section

in loving memory of Robert and Jane Townsley
and of their daughters Carrie Donaldson and Winnie
United

TRIMBLE	black marble stone	A-2 Section

TRIMBLE
in loving memory of a devoted wife and mother
Agnes (Nennie) died 17 July 1979

TRIMBLE	stone and surround	A-5 Section

TRIMBLE
erected by Sarah Trimble in memory of her beloved husband
George James Trimble who died 28 May 1930 also the above named
Sarah Trimble who died 23 February 1975

TURNER	small black vase	No 057 OLD Section

Joe Turner died 18.2.57

TURNER	see Tierney	No 168A OLD Section

TURVILL	see Gilmore	A-1 Section
UNKNOWN	no stone	No 003 OLD Section
UNKNOWN	no stone	No 006 OLD Section
UNKNOWN	no stone	No 008 OLD Section
UNKNOWN	no stone	No 012 OLD Section
UNKNOWN	no stone	No 029 OLD Section
UNKNOWN	no stone	No 036 OLD Section
UNKNOWN	no stone	No 041 OLD Section
UNKNOWN	no stone	No 043 OLD Section
UNKNOWN	no stone	No 053C OLD Section
UNKNOWN	no stone	No 056 OLD Section
UNKNOWN	no stone	No 062 OLD Section
UNKNOWN	no stone	No 067 OLD Section
UNKNOWN	no stone	No 076 OLD Section
UNKNOWN	no stone	No 080 OLD Section
UNKNOWN	no stone	No 083 OLD Section
UNKNOWN	no stone	No 085 OLD Section
UNKNOWN	no stone	No 089 OLD Section
UNKNOWN	no stone	No 100 OLD Section
UNKNOWN	no stone	No 107 OLD Section
UNKNOWN	no stone or plot with this number	No 115 OLD Section

UNKNOWN	fallen stone too heavy to be lifted	No 116 OLD Section
UNKNOWN	no stone	No 118 OLD Section
UNKNOWN	no stone	No 125 OLD Section
UNKNOWN	no stone	No 127 OLD Section
UNKNOWN	no stone	No 139 OLD Section
UNKNOWN	no stone	No 141A OLD Section
UNKNOWN	no stone	No 144A OLD Section
UNKNOWN	no stone	No 158 OLD Section
UNKNOWN	no stone	No 166 OLD Section
UNKNOWN	no stone	No 180 OLD Section
WALKER	grey stone and surround	A-2 Section

WALKER
in loving memory of my dear husband and our dear father
James died 21 July 1955
Love's last gift, remembrance

WALKER	black urn	A-5 Section

WALKER
Harriet 25 May 1973

WALKER	black square pillar with vase	A-12 Section

erected by K.G.Walker
in loving memory of his wife
Agnes Elizabeth who died 12 September 1900 aged 39 years also his son
George A McCartney who died 11 June 1884 ? aged 7 months and his son
George who died 7 April 1923 aged 37 years and
Kirker who died 20 January 1927 aged 35 years
the above named
K.G.Walker died 24 August 1933 aged 75 years
Vase Mum and Dad
Right side
Mary Jane Walker died 17 July 1977
beloved wife of Bartholomew died 29 August 1993
Left side
Maud beloved wife of James T. Walker who died 4 February 1919 aged 32 years
the above James T. Walker died 15 May 1967

WALKER	grey granite	A-13 Section

WALKER
in memory of my loving parents
Arthur died 27 July 1985
Elizabeth died 22 February 1986

WALKER	see Crawford	No 016 OLD Section

| WALKER | no stone | No 068 OLD Section |

on map - Wm J Walker

| WALKER | tall granite stone | No 104 OLD Section |

erected by Thomas Walker of Belfast in memory of his children
Margaret died 29 April 1856 aged 14 years
John, Elizabeth, Sarah, Robert, Thomas and Sarah who all died young
Thomas Walker born 28 May 1813 died 14 June 1890 also
Margaret his wife born 30 June 1821 died 10 April 1894 and his daughter
Mary Jane Walker born 1 February 1850 died 9 February 1917
on map - Tom Sands

| WALKER | limestone headstone | No 104A OLD Section |

in memory of John Walker of Shaneshill who died 13 May 1845 AE 80 years also
Elizabeth his wife who died 1 December 1822 aged 38 years also their son
Joseph who died August 20 1838 ae 38 years also their son
John who died 3 July 1857 aged 48 years
on map - Mary J Walker

| WALLACE | stone and surround | A-2 Section |

in loving memory of my beloved husband
James Wallace much loved father of Berta and Lottie
died 8 October 1932 also his wife
Annie Jane died 15 April 1971
Resting
WALLACE

| WARWICK | see Bigger | No 015C OLD Section |

| WATSON | black marble stone | A-12 Section |

WATSON

| WATSON ? | white chain enclosure and vase | A-7 Section |

in loving memory of mother
Wooden cross   WATS..

| WATT | white marble stone and surround | A-8 Section |

WATT
in loving memory of our dear sons
James Watt died 18 February 1921
Samuel Watt died 20 December 1923 also our dear daughter
Margaret Lewis died 11 April 1943

| WATT | see Kelso | No 024 OLD Section |

| WAUGH | marble and surround | A-13 Section |

WAUGH
in loving memory of a dear husband and devoted father
John Allen died 23 April 1972 also my dear and only daughter
Sally died 5 September 1975 aged 21 years
Worthy of everlasting remembrance

| WEBB | see Kelso | No 009 OLD Section |

| WILKINSON | no stone | No 150 OLD Section |

on map - Isabella Wilkinson

| WILLIAMSON | white marble and railings | A-6 Section |

WILLIAMSON
in loving memory of
John A. Williamson died 23 March 1955 aged 82 years, his wife
Margaret Jane Williamson died 3 April 1958 aged 92 years
Margaret Elizabeth Williamson died 6 November 1972 aged 73 years

---

| WILLIAMSON | see Green | No 026 OLD Section |

| WILLIAMSON | limestone headstone | No 134 OLD Section |

erected by Mary Williamson of Craigarogan in memory of her father
John Dollar who died 31 December 1876 aged 90 years also his wife
Isabella who died 29 January 1837 aged 54 years also
Thomas Kirkwood died 24 March 1916
on map - Jean A Finney, Mrs Williamson and John Dollar

| WILLIAMSON | white marble - decorated top | No 160 OLD Section |

erected by Martha Williamson in loving memory of her mother
Mary Williamson who departed this life 11 July 1901 aged 82 years also her
father Matthew Williamson who departed this life 18 March 1905 aged 92 years
John Williamson died 6 July 1966
on map - John Williamson

| WILSON | small stone in railings | A-4 Section |

in loving memory of my dear husband
James Wilson died 10 August 1926 also my son
Robert J died 19 January 1932

| WILSON | white marble stone & surround | A-6 Section |

WILSON
in loving memory of a devoted husband and father
Thomas Wilson who died 7 September 1958 also his dear wife
Alice Maud Wilson who died 10 May 1972

| WILSON | large granite plot | A-8 Section |

WILSON
the family burying ground of Thomas Wilson

| WILSON | black vase | A-8 Section |

WILSON

| WILSON | large stone and surround | A-12 Section |

1908
erected to the memory of
David Wilson, Physician and surgeon of Notting Hill, Whiteabbey
who died 5 October 1908 aged 67 years also his sister
Elizabeth Wilson who died 17 July 1903 aged 63 years also his nephew
David Wilson, Physician and surgeon of Notting Hill, Whiteabbey
who died 5 February 1956 aged 83 years also wife of above
Elizabeth Dundee Adams Wilson who died 20 March 1965 aged 88 years
also daughter of the above Muriel Elizabeth Wilson
who died 10 August 1980 aged 76 years
WILSON

| WILSON | marble stone and surround | A-12 Section |

in loving memory of my dear wife
Isabella who died 9 October 1955 also her dear husband
Gordon who died 21 January 1970
WILSON

| WILSON | grey marble stone and surround | A-12 Section |

WILSON
in loving memory of Thomas Wilson, Ballyvesey
who died 24 February 1931 aged 82 years also his wife
Isabella who died 29 May 1941 aged 90 years, their son
James who died 31 December 1956 aged 82 years, his wife
Elizabeth who died 28 July 1958 aged 78 years
At rest
Left edge
his son Robert who died 5 October 1931 aged 55 years

| WILSON | black marble | A-13 Section |

WILSON
Robert James died 12 august 1987

| WILSON | grey stone | A-14 Section |

WILSON
in loving memory of Alexander 1905 - 1991
beloved husband of May and father of Derrick

| WILSON | see Russell | No 122B OLD Section |

| WILSON | see Sherrard | No 124C OLD Section |

| WILSON | see Sherrard | No 124D OLD Section |

| WILSON | see Speer | No 140A OLD Section |

| WILSON | limestone - decorated top | No 147 OLD Section |

erected by Robert Wilson of Ballyvesey
as a tribute of regard to the memory of his uncle
James Ferguson who departed this life 15 April 1825 aged 69 years also the
said Robert Wilson who died 10 April 1849 aged 44 years also his wife
Jane who died 19 November 1875 aged 67 years also his grandson
David died 23 July 1894 aged 16 years
Janet Wilson died 29 August 1926
William John Wilson died 20 April 1930
Henry R Wilson died 16 January 1945
on map - H Wilson

| WILSON | no stone | No 154 OLD Section |

on map - Wilson

| WINCHESTER | see Skelly | A-6 Section |

| WINTERS | white marble stone and surround | A-6 Section |

WINTERS
in loving memory of my dear brother
Joseph called home 16 April 1960
Walter loving husband of Gretta died 5 April 1970 also
Frederick died 6 October 1986
Severed only till He come

| WINTERS | white stone and railings | A-8 Section |

in loving memory of my dear husband
Joseph Winters who departed this life 7 May 1927 also my darling children
Willie and Greta and dearly loved grandchildren also his beloved wife
Margaret Winters who fell asleep 10 June 1949
Thy will be done

WISEMAN	see Compton	A-10 Section

WITHERS	black marble stone and surround	A-12 Section

WITHERS
Moirin 1916 - 1987
dearly beloved wife of Kenneth
She enriched life in love, care and family joy
Left side
James Withers 1848-1903
Vase Moirin 19 March 1987

WOODS	marble stone and surround	A-8 Section

WOODS
in loving memory of
James Woods who died 11 November 1914, his wife
Agnes who died 26 January 1926, their sons
Matthew James who died 5 October 1928
William David who died 17 March 1960, their daughter
Annie Boyd who died 7 September 1951
and was interred in 2nd Ballyeaston Churchyard, their son-on-law
Hugh Beggs who died 17 August 1953, their daughter
Mary Agnes Beggs who died 5 April 1981
Left side
Mary A McDowell who died 18 July 1988

WRIGHT	see Martin	A-2 Section

WYLIE	see Boston	A-2 Section

WYLIE	stone and iron surround	A-5 Section

WYLIE
in loving memory of
Margaret who died 12 November 1937 also her beloved husband
William Hugh who died 1 March 1957
Absent from the body
At home, O Lord, with Thee
white vase - WYLIE

WYLIE	see McCallum	A-8 Section

WYLIE	black marble and surround	A-13 Section

WYLIE
in loving memory of Cecil Walsley died 2 November 1972

YOUNG	large grey granite stone	A-5 Section

YOUNG
in remembrance of Robert Young, Granard, Whiteabbey
died 1 April 1946 also his beloved wife
Jane Lindsay Young died 5 August 1950 also their dear son
Robert died 22 November 1994

NOTES